Proper Education Group

4 Practice Tests for the Texas Real Estate Exam

"The secret to getting ahead is getting started."
Mark Twain

Table of Contents

Introduction

1.1 Requirements

On the day of the test, you must bring the following:

1. **TWO** forms of valid and non-expired government-issued ID with a valid signature. One must be government issued and include a photo. Examples include:
   a. Driver's license
   b. State issued identification (ex. non-driver ID)
   c. United States Passport
   d. Credit card
2. A second ID that contains your signature and legal name
3. A basic non-scientific calculator

You are not required to bring a calculator, but you are **highly encouraged to do so** as there will be simple mathematical questions that require multiplication and division. Do not rely on the one on your phone because **phones will not be allowed**.

1.2 About the Exam

The test is 180 minutes long and composed of two sections.

The national portion is composed of 85 multiple choice questions and the time limit is 150 minutes. You must answer at least 56 of 85 questions correctly to pass the national portion.

The state portion is composed of 40 multiple choice questions and the time limit is 90 minutes. You must answer at least 21 of 40 questions correctly to pass the state portion.

The exam is administered through a computer.

1.3 How to Apply

To apply for the exam, visit the website below and submit the required the forms:

https://mylicense.trec.texas.gov/datamart/registration.do

All of the official documentation pertaining payments, documents, and forms can be found there.

Alternatively, you may also apply by filling out the paper form here:

https://www.trec.texas.gov/forms/application-inactive-real-estate-sales-agent-license

1.4 Exam Results

Your score will be given to you immediately after finishing the exam

Practice Test 1

Directions:

1. You have a 150-minute time limit for the national portion, and a 90-minute time limit for the state portion.

2. To pass, you must answer at least 56 out of 85 questions correctly on the national portion **AND** at least 21 out of 40 questions on the state portion.

3. Some questions will require mathematics. You may use a calculator.

4. **Phones and pagers are not allowed. Having either will result in automatic dismissal from the exam and nullification of exam scores.**

Tips:

- Answer all questions even if you are unsure.
- Mark any questions you are stuck on and revisit them after you are done. The exam is timed so make sure you finish as many questions as you can.
- After reading the question, try answering it in your head first to avoid getting confused by the choices.
- Read the entire question before looking at the answers.
- Use the process of elimination to filter out choices that don't seem correct to increase your chances of selecting the correct answer.
- Be aware of important keywords like **not, sometimes, always,** and **never**. These words completely alter the ask of the question so it's important to keep track of them.

PLEASE READ THESE INSTRUCTIONS CAREFULLY.

Name: _____   Date: _____

NATIONAL PORTION

1.	Ⓐ	Ⓑ	Ⓒ	Ⓓ	31.	Ⓐ	Ⓑ	Ⓒ	Ⓓ	61.	Ⓐ	Ⓑ	Ⓒ	Ⓓ
2.	Ⓐ	Ⓑ	Ⓒ	Ⓓ	32.	Ⓐ	Ⓑ	Ⓒ	Ⓓ	62.	Ⓐ	Ⓑ	Ⓒ	Ⓓ
3.	Ⓐ	Ⓑ	Ⓒ	Ⓓ	33.	Ⓐ	Ⓑ	Ⓒ	Ⓓ	63.	Ⓐ	Ⓑ	Ⓒ	Ⓓ
4.	Ⓐ	Ⓑ	Ⓒ	Ⓓ	34.	Ⓐ	Ⓑ	Ⓒ	Ⓓ	64.	Ⓐ	Ⓑ	Ⓒ	Ⓓ
5.	Ⓐ	Ⓑ	Ⓒ	Ⓓ	35.	Ⓐ	Ⓑ	Ⓒ	Ⓓ	65.	Ⓐ	Ⓑ	Ⓒ	Ⓓ
6.	Ⓐ	Ⓑ	Ⓒ	Ⓓ	36.	Ⓐ	Ⓑ	Ⓒ	Ⓓ	66.	Ⓐ	Ⓑ	Ⓒ	Ⓓ
7.	Ⓐ	Ⓑ	Ⓒ	Ⓓ	37.	Ⓐ	Ⓑ	Ⓒ	Ⓓ	67.	Ⓐ	Ⓑ	Ⓒ	Ⓓ
8.	Ⓐ	Ⓑ	Ⓒ	Ⓓ	38.	Ⓐ	Ⓑ	Ⓒ	Ⓓ	68.	Ⓐ	Ⓑ	Ⓒ	Ⓓ
9.	Ⓐ	Ⓑ	Ⓒ	Ⓓ	39.	Ⓐ	Ⓑ	Ⓒ	Ⓓ	69.	Ⓐ	Ⓑ	Ⓒ	Ⓓ
10.	Ⓐ	Ⓑ	Ⓒ	Ⓓ	40.	Ⓐ	Ⓑ	Ⓒ	Ⓓ	70.	Ⓐ	Ⓑ	Ⓒ	Ⓓ
11.	Ⓐ	Ⓑ	Ⓒ	Ⓓ	41.	Ⓐ	Ⓑ	Ⓒ	Ⓓ	71.	Ⓐ	Ⓑ	Ⓒ	Ⓓ
12.	Ⓐ	Ⓑ	Ⓒ	Ⓓ	42.	Ⓐ	Ⓑ	Ⓒ	Ⓓ	72.	Ⓐ	Ⓑ	Ⓒ	Ⓓ
13.	Ⓐ	Ⓑ	Ⓒ	Ⓓ	43.	Ⓐ	Ⓑ	Ⓒ	Ⓓ	73.	Ⓐ	Ⓑ	Ⓒ	Ⓓ
14.	Ⓐ	Ⓑ	Ⓒ	Ⓓ	44.	Ⓐ	Ⓑ	Ⓒ	Ⓓ	74.	Ⓐ	Ⓑ	Ⓒ	Ⓓ
15.	Ⓐ	Ⓑ	Ⓒ	Ⓓ	45.	Ⓐ	Ⓑ	Ⓒ	Ⓓ	75.	Ⓐ	Ⓑ	Ⓒ	Ⓓ
16.	Ⓐ	Ⓑ	Ⓒ	Ⓓ	46.	Ⓐ	Ⓑ	Ⓒ	Ⓓ	76.	Ⓐ	Ⓑ	Ⓒ	Ⓓ
17	Ⓐ	Ⓑ	Ⓒ	Ⓓ	47.	Ⓐ	Ⓑ	Ⓒ	Ⓓ	77.	Ⓐ	Ⓑ	Ⓒ	Ⓓ
18.	Ⓐ	Ⓑ	Ⓒ	Ⓓ	48.	Ⓐ	Ⓑ	Ⓒ	Ⓓ	78.	Ⓐ	Ⓑ	Ⓒ	Ⓓ
19.	Ⓐ	Ⓑ	Ⓒ	Ⓓ	49.	Ⓐ	Ⓑ	Ⓒ	Ⓓ	79.	Ⓐ	Ⓑ	Ⓒ	Ⓓ
20.	Ⓐ	Ⓑ	Ⓒ	Ⓓ	50.	Ⓐ	Ⓑ	Ⓒ	Ⓓ	80.	Ⓐ	Ⓑ	Ⓒ	Ⓓ
21.	Ⓐ	Ⓑ	Ⓒ	Ⓓ	51.	Ⓐ	Ⓑ	Ⓒ	Ⓓ	81.	Ⓐ	Ⓑ	Ⓒ	Ⓓ
22.	Ⓐ	Ⓑ	Ⓒ	Ⓓ	52.	Ⓐ	Ⓑ	Ⓒ	Ⓓ	82.	Ⓐ	Ⓑ	Ⓒ	Ⓓ
23.	Ⓐ	Ⓑ	Ⓒ	Ⓓ	53.	Ⓐ	Ⓑ	Ⓒ	Ⓓ	83.	Ⓐ	Ⓑ	Ⓒ	Ⓓ
24.	Ⓐ	Ⓑ	Ⓒ	Ⓓ	54.	Ⓐ	Ⓑ	Ⓒ	Ⓓ	84.	Ⓐ	Ⓑ	Ⓒ	Ⓓ
25.	Ⓐ	Ⓑ	Ⓒ	Ⓓ	55.	Ⓐ	Ⓑ	Ⓒ	Ⓓ	85.	Ⓐ	Ⓑ	Ⓒ	Ⓓ
26.	Ⓐ	Ⓑ	Ⓒ	Ⓓ	56.	Ⓐ	Ⓑ	Ⓒ	Ⓓ					
27.	Ⓐ	Ⓑ	Ⓒ	Ⓓ	57.	Ⓐ	Ⓑ	Ⓒ	Ⓓ					
28.	Ⓐ	Ⓑ	Ⓒ	Ⓓ	58.	Ⓐ	Ⓑ	Ⓒ	Ⓓ					
29.	Ⓐ	Ⓑ	Ⓒ	Ⓓ	59.	Ⓐ	Ⓑ	Ⓒ	Ⓓ					
30.	Ⓐ	Ⓑ	Ⓒ	Ⓓ	60.	Ⓐ	Ⓑ	Ⓒ	Ⓓ					

Name: _____   Date: _____

STATE PORTION

1.   Ⓐ Ⓑ Ⓒ Ⓓ   31.   Ⓐ Ⓑ Ⓒ Ⓓ
2.   Ⓐ Ⓑ Ⓒ Ⓓ   32.   Ⓐ Ⓑ Ⓒ Ⓓ
3.   Ⓐ Ⓑ Ⓒ Ⓓ   33.   Ⓐ Ⓑ Ⓒ Ⓓ
4.   Ⓐ Ⓑ Ⓒ Ⓓ   34.   Ⓐ Ⓑ Ⓒ Ⓓ
5.   Ⓐ Ⓑ Ⓒ Ⓓ   35.   Ⓐ Ⓑ Ⓒ Ⓓ
6.   Ⓐ Ⓑ Ⓒ Ⓓ   36.   Ⓐ Ⓑ Ⓒ Ⓓ
7.   Ⓐ Ⓑ Ⓒ Ⓓ   37.   Ⓐ Ⓑ Ⓒ Ⓓ
8.   Ⓐ Ⓑ Ⓒ Ⓓ   38.   Ⓐ Ⓑ Ⓒ Ⓓ
9.   Ⓐ Ⓑ Ⓒ Ⓓ   39.   Ⓐ Ⓑ Ⓒ Ⓓ
10. Ⓐ Ⓑ Ⓒ Ⓓ   40.   Ⓐ Ⓑ Ⓒ Ⓓ
11. Ⓐ Ⓑ Ⓒ Ⓓ
12. Ⓐ Ⓑ Ⓒ Ⓓ
13. Ⓐ Ⓑ Ⓒ Ⓓ
14. Ⓐ Ⓑ Ⓒ Ⓓ
15. Ⓐ Ⓑ Ⓒ Ⓓ
16. Ⓐ Ⓑ Ⓒ Ⓓ
17   Ⓐ Ⓑ Ⓒ Ⓓ
18. Ⓐ Ⓑ Ⓒ Ⓓ
19. Ⓐ Ⓑ Ⓒ Ⓓ
20. Ⓐ Ⓑ Ⓒ Ⓓ
21. Ⓐ Ⓑ Ⓒ Ⓓ
22. Ⓐ Ⓑ Ⓒ Ⓓ
23. Ⓐ Ⓑ Ⓒ Ⓓ
24. Ⓐ Ⓑ Ⓒ Ⓓ
25. Ⓐ Ⓑ Ⓒ Ⓓ
26. Ⓐ Ⓑ Ⓒ Ⓓ
27. Ⓐ Ⓑ Ⓒ Ⓓ
28. Ⓐ Ⓑ Ⓒ Ⓓ
29. Ⓐ Ⓑ Ⓒ Ⓓ
30. Ⓐ Ⓑ Ⓒ Ⓓ

NATIONAL PORTION

1. When applying for a loan, what is a **fixed rate**?

   A. A loan that has a predetermined repayment interest rate
   B. A loan whose interest rates do not change throughout the life of the loan
   C. A loan that accrues no interest
   D. A loan that pays off the interest before the principal

2. What act prohibits discrimination based on race or color?

   A. Fair Housing Act
   B. Civil Rights Act of 1866
   C. Civil Right Act of 1964
   D. Civil Rights Act Amendment of 1974

3. What is the financial document that contains a written promise to fulfill a certain payment?

   A. Invoice
   B. Promissory note
   C. Pro forma statement
   D. IOU

4. What is the term used to describe the act of replacing an existing mortgage with another?

   A. Refinancing
   B. Defaulting
   C. Foreclosure
   D. Reinvesting

5. Which is **not** an appurtenant right?

   A. Furnace
   B. Swimming pool
   C. Air conditioning
   D. All of the above

6. What is the name given to the banking option that allows a customer to deposit a specified amount for a predetermined period of time?

   A. Certificate of occupation
   B. Certificate of deposit
   C. Investment clause
   D. Mortgage

7. If a seller nets $225,000 after paying a 10% fee, what was the total he received?

   A. $202,500
   B. $224,990
   C. $250,000
   D. None of the above

8. What is the name given to the rate earned for borrowing or an investment per year?

   A. Rate lock
   B. Fixed rate
   C. Floating rate
   D. Annual percentage rate

9. Other than buying a home using traditional channels, what other methods can a prospective owner use to buy a home?

   A. Public auctions
   B. Tender
   C. Lease
   D. Escalation clause

10. What is the reviewing of a borrower's credit worthiness prior to loan approval?

   A. Buydown
   B. Pre-qualification
   C. Credit score
   D. Under qualification

11. What is the document that is used to transfer legal rights to act in the interest of a person?

   A. Disclosure form
   B. Power of attorney
   C. Pro forma statement
   D. Deed

12. What type of listing only guarantees commission for a sale within a specified period?

   A. Exclusive listing
   B. Net listing
   C. Single agency listing
   D. Multi agency listing

13. What type of brokerage mandates that the broker acts in the best interest of the buyer?

   A. Single agency
   B. Dual agency
   C. Multi agency
   D. Full service

14. What is the name of a transaction where both the buyer and seller are seeking the best deal?

   A. Real estate transaction
   B. Credit transaction
   C. Arms-length transaction
   D. Debited transaction

15. What is the name given to modification of billing calculation dates?

   A. Modified date
   B. Closing date
   C. Opening date
   D. Adjustment date

16. What is the name of the mortgage that is transferred by the seller to the buyer?

   A. Assumable mortgage
   B. Adjusted rate mortgage
   C. Fixed rate mortgage
   D. Floating mortgage

17. What is the contract that secures a future transaction?

    A.   Deed
    B.   Call option
    C.   Title
    D.   None of the above

18. What does an exclusive listing contract need to be considered valid?

    A.   A net listing
    B.   A commission rate of at least 6%
    C.   A specified expiration date
    D.   The signature of the grantee

19. What is it when another state recognizes your real estate license?

    A.   Transfer
    B.   Limited basis policy
    C.   Reciprocity
    D.   None of the above

20. Which of the following is **not** a fiduciary duty?

    A.   Accounting
    B.   Confidentiality
    C.   Obedience
    D.   Privacy

21. What are contingencies as used in real estate?

    A.   Conditions that must be met by both the buyer and the seller before closing
    B.   Conditions set by the government on buying a home
    C.   Conditions set by the bank in order to approve a loan for a mortgage
    D.   Conditions that must be met to avoid judicial foreclosure

22. Who is a co-borrower?

    A.   Any individual whose name appears on the loan document
    B.   Someone that borrows money at the same time with you
    C.   The mortgage broker that originates the loan for you
    D.   An individual that guarantees your loan

23. What is the name given to a loan taken out to finance construction?

    A.   Mortgage
    B.   Construction loan
    C.   Business loan
    D.   Personal loan

24. What is the name given to the inspection done by the buyer before closing?

    A.   Final inspection
    B.   Advertorial
    C.   Housing ratio
    D.   Final walkthrough

25. What is the name given to a mortgage whose interest rate does **not** change throughout the payment period?

   A. Adjustable mortgage rate
   B. Floating rate
   C. Fixed mortgage rate
   D. Bridge loan

26. What is defined as the percentage owned by the buyer after making a down payment?

   A. Housing ratio
   B. Debt to income ratio
   C. Loan to value ratio
   D. Floating rate

27. What is the cash on cash return of a $60,000 investment that generates $1,000 in monthly cash flow?

   A. 1.67%
   B. 2%
   C. 20%
   D. None of the above

28. What is the term used to refer to the responsibility one individual has for the acts of another?

   A. Vicarious liability
   B. Fixed liability
   C. Current liability
   D. Contingent

29. What is the name given to a form used to explain the role of an agent in a real estate transaction?

   A. Purchase agreement
   B. Accountability
   C. Assignment contract
   D. Agency disclosure statement

30. A number of brokers agreed on a set standard commission. What antitrust law are they guilty of violating?

   A. Commingling
   B. Price fixing
   C. Steering
   D. Discussing

31. Which government agency is responsible for determining the status of an independent contractor?

   A. Federal government
   B. Bank
   C. Department of State
   D. IRS

32. What is the nature of the title issued in condo ownership?

   A. Freehold
   B. Regular
   C. Deed
   D. Clear title

33. Mr. and Mrs. Johnson made a $350,000 profit on the sale of their primary home. How much do they owe in capital gains tax?

   A. $0
   B. $3,500
   C. $50,000
   D. Half of the amount earned

34. What is the status of an agent's license once it is revoked?

   A. Pending
   B. Cancelled
   C. Breached
   D. Suspended

35. Which insurance policy provides extra liability coverage for the insured party?

   A. Umbrella policy
   B. Home insurance
   C. Flood insurance
   D. Hazard insurance

36. What is never included in the process of valuation?

   A. Comparative Market Analysis
   B. Appraisal
   C. Location
   D. Condition of the house

37. What type of contract allows the parties involved to disaffirm without liability?

   A. Bilateral contract
   B. Implied contract
   C. Unilateral contract
   D. Voidable Contract

38. What fiduciary duty does a broker neglect by failing to disclosing the buyer's inability to afford a down payment?

   A. Obedience
   B. Disclosure
   C. Accountability
   D. Confidentiality

39. James and Peter co-own a property where they both have equal undivided interests and right of survivorship. What co-ownership agreement do they have?

   A. Tenancy in entirety
   B. Joint tenancy
   C. Tenancy in common
   D. Tenancy at will

40. What is an exclusive term to describe the lease entered when an individual buys shares from a housing corporation?

   A. Percentage lease
   B. Gross lease
   C. Net lease
   D. Proprietary lease

41. What is the state of having no legal effect?

    A.   Enforceable
    B.   Cancelled
    C.   Void
    D.   Terminated

42. How many square feet constitute an acre?

    A.   25,235
    B.   43,560
    C.   50,525
    D.   70,000

43. What is the set minimum amp for a new construction?

    A.   100 amps
    B.   150 amps
    C.   200 amps
    D.   250 amps

44. What is the debt-to-equity ratio on a mortgage valued at $1,000,000 with a loan of $750,000?

    A.   25%
    B.   50%
    C.   65%
    D.   75%

45. Who controls flood insurance?

    A.   FEMA
    B.   EPA
    C.   CERCLA
    D.   FHA

46. What is a detailed building plan that is needed before starting construction?

    A.   Building design
    B.   Execution plan
    C.   Blueprint
    D.   Authorized plan

47. What type of house insulation was banned due to the release of formaldehyde fumes?

    A.   Foam boards
    B.   Loose fill
    C.   Vapor barriers
    D.   UFFI

48. What is the term used to describe a scenario where an agent represents both the buyer and the seller?

    A.   Single agency
    B.   Dual agency
    C.   Multi agency
    D.   Representing both agency

49. Which formal agreement gives an agent the sole right to sell a property?

    A. Purchase agreement
    B. Floating rate
    C. Fixed mortgage rate
    D. Bridge loan

50. A tenant is legally allowed to remove equipment previously installed to facilitate business operations before the expiry of a lease. Why is this the case?

    A. The equipment is considered trade fixtures
    B. The equipment belongs to the lease holder
    C. The lessor does not want it
    D. It was part of the lease agreement

51. What type of easement attaches rights to an individual rather than the property?

    A. Easement appurtenant
    B. Easement in gross
    C. Prescriptive easement
    D. All of the above

52. What is the name given to the lowest section of the roof that extends into the sidewalls?

    A. Board
    B. Shingles
    C. Joists
    D. Beams

53. Which two parties are responsible for determining the commission earned by the broker?

    A. Seller and agent
    B. Seller and broker
    C. Buyer and agent
    D. Buyer and seller

54. Why must a lawsuit be filed within a specific time after an occurrence?

    A. To prevent the criminal from getting away
    B. Lis pendens
    C. Credibility
    D. Statute of limitations

55. Chris borrows money to purchase a new home and gives the mortgage to the lender as security. What term can be used to refer to Chris?

    A. Mortgagor
    B. Mortgagee
    C. Broker
    D. Buyer

56. What type of lease does a tenant have when he is paying a percentage of gross sales in addition to the base rent?

    A. Proprietary lease
    B. Net lease
    C. Percentage lease
    D. Gross lease

57. Why was the Civil Rights Act of 1866 significant in real estate?

    A. It protected against racial discrimination

    B. It protected interests of women

    C. It protected children's rights

    D. It protected against ageism

58. Why was the Privacy Act of 1974 significant?

    A. It required agencies to publicize records to the Federal Register

    B. It required privacy of records

    C. It required federal government to operate without transparency

    D. It required credit information to be kept private

59. Why was the Civil Liberties Act of 1988 significant?

    A. It granted all citizens equality

    B. It granted reparations to Japanese Americans interned by the government during World War II

    C. It passed rights to empower women in employment

    D. It passed rights to ensure fair housing

60. Jack is trying to convince Mary to sell her property in her neighborhood because it is changing due to the influx of people of other ethnic backgrounds. What is he doing?

    A. Steering

    B. Discriminating

    C. Blockbusting

    D. Convincing

61. What is the name of an agreement that allows for conditions on a property?

    A. Contract

    B. Deed

    C. Lease

    D. Qualified fee estate

62. What is **redlining**?

    A. Refusal by lending institutions to grant loans based on race

    B. Refusal by lending institutions to grant loans to people with poor credit scores

    C. Refusal of lending institutions to grant loans based on the agency being used for a purchase

    D. Refusal of a lending institution to make a loan because the area is integrated or populated by culturally diverse people

63. What is a form of co-ownership that involves a husband and wife having equal and undivided interest in the property?

    A. Joint tenancy

    B. Tenancy in common

    C. Tenancy by entirety

    D. Tenancy at will

64. What is the act of a property reverting to the state on death of the owner?

    A. Escheat

    B. Encumbrance

    C. Easement

    D. Suing

65. If you have a loan of $150,000 with an 8% interest, how much do you pay in interest every month?

    A. $1,000
    B. $1,200
    C. $5,000
    D. $12,000

66. Based on their contract, a lender declares the entire balance of the loan due immediately due to default by the borrower. How is this possible?

    A.   Payday loans
    B.   Alternative financing
    C.   Acceleration clause
    D.   Lines of credit

67. What type of payment plan allows a borrower to make smaller payments in the early years of a mortgage with payments increasing over time?

    A.   Blanket mortgage
    B.   Graduated mortgage
    C.   Anomalous mortgage
    D.   Balloon mortgage

68. What kind of mortgage should you apply for if you are buying more than an individual unit or plot?

    A.   Graduated mortgage
    B.   Blanket mortgage
    C.   Balloon mortgage
    D.   Adjustable rate mortgage

69. A salesperson is presented with two offers on a listed property. One is above the listing price and another below, which offer should he present to the seller?

    A.   Both offers
    B.   The one above the listing price
    C.   The one below the listing price
    D.   Neither

70. What is the name of a transaction where a seller finances the whole sale or part of the sale of a property for the buyer?

    A.   Mortgage
    B.   Refinancing
    C.   Purchase money
    D.   Buydown

71. What is an assessment of the value of a property as of a specific date based on objective data?

    A.   CMA
    B.   Listing price
    C.   Tax value
    D.   Appraisal

72. Which toxic metallic element is found in old paint and water pipes?

    A.   Mercury
    B.   Manganese
    C.   Cadmium
    D.   Lead

73. What is the amount of space used to calculate the lease payments which includes the shared property's common and service areas?

   A. Rentable square footage
   B. Usable square footage
   C. Common areas
   D. Service areas

74. Which chemical compounds commonly used in coolants and refrigeration contribute to the depletion of the ozone?

   A. CFCs
   B. Tetrafluoroethane
   C. Anhydrous ammonia
   D. Greenhouse gases

75. Which of the following does liability insurance protect you from?

   A. House fire
   B. Injury incurred on property
   C. Flood
   D. All of the above

76. What is a deed used for?

   A. To transfer title rights
   B. An official document proving a bank has loaned money
   C. A pro forma statement
   D. A lien

77. What is the measurement used to show the volatility of a market?

   A. Absorption rate
   B. Fluctuation rate
   C. Inflation
   D. Purchase deviation

78. What is the relationship between a broker and their client called?

   A. Fiduciary
   B. Trustee
   C. Seller disclosure
   D. Subagent

79. What is the law of agency?

   A. Commissions that are collected from both parties
   B. A set of laws that apply to a person who acts on behalf of another person
   C. The ability to accept an offer on behalf of the seller
   D. An authorized agency selling another's property

80. A severance is defined as _____.

   A. Real property that is converted into personal property
   B. Anything that is attached to the property naturally or by a person
   C. A person that is acting under a power of attorney
   D. An agreement between a lender and a borrower in which the borrower pledges collateral on a loan

81. _____ is the increase in value that occurs when combining two parcels into one large parcel.

   A. Redlining
   B. Plottage
   C. Assemblage
   D. Due diligence

82. What is a traffic report?

   A. A. A list of property's a broker is selling at one time
   B. A list of property that have been listed for sale in a specified area
   C. The number of property's a licensed broker is managing
   D. A list of prospects who have inquired or visited the property

83. What is the purpose of the Real Estate Settlement and Procedures Act?

   A. Provide buyers and sellers with disclosures regarding settlement costs
   B. Protect licensed brokers and agents from abusive practices regarding settlements
   C. Ensure buyers and sellers have the ability to back out of settlements within 30 days
   D. Pursue lawsuits against licensed brokers and agents on behalf of the client

84. _____ is also referred to as panic selling or panic peddling.

   A. Redlining
   B. Blockbusting
   C. Amortization
   D. Easement

85. A liability that consists of smaller payments of interest and principal and a balloon payment on the loan maturity date is a
_____.

 A. Term loan
 B. Fully amortized loan
 C. Partially amortized loan
 D. Balloon loan

THIS IS THE END OF THE NATIONAL PORTION.

STATE PORTION

1. How many members are there on the Texas Real Estate Commission (TREC)

    A. 9
    B. 3
    C. 6
    D. 7

2. Texas requires a salesperson to _____ if they wish to sell their personal real estate.

    A. They are not allowed to sell their own real estate
    B. Get approval from the TREC
    C. Disclose, in writing, their intent to sell their own property
    D. They do not have to do anything

3. How much can a licensed salesperson pay a customer who refers a buyer to that salesperson?

    A. 5% of the sale
    B. A flat fee no higher than $500,00
    C. The customer and salesperson can negotiate a payment
    D. A salesperson cannot pay an unlicensed customer

4. What does the acronym MUD mean?

    A. Mortgage under duress
    B. Municipal utility district
    C. Municipal under default
    D. None of the above

5. Texas requires earnest money to be deposited into a trust account within _____ days.

    A. 10 business days
    B. 3 business days
    C. 2 business days
    D. 1 business day

6. How long is the option period for real estate transactions conducted in Texas?

    A. The option period is negotiable
    B. 48 hours
    C. 10 days
    D. 7 days

7. What is the penalty for participating in real estate transactions without a license?

    A. Administrative penalty
    B. A complaint from TREC
    C. Cease and desist
    D. All of the above

8. How long does a broker need to keep real estate and financial documents?

    A. 3 years
    B. 4 years
    C. 5 years
    D. 7 years

9. According to the Texas Property Tax Exemptions, a family can have one homestead of up to _____ in a rural area in the state of Texas.

   A. 100 acres
   B. 150 acres
   C. 200 acres
   D. 50 acres

10. How many hours of core real estate classes does a licensee need to complete to renew their license?

   A. 18 hours
   B. 10 hours
   C. 8 hours
   D. 6 hours

11. The _____ allows a buyer to terminate a contract and collect the earnest money if the lender determines the property fails to satisfy the underwriting requirements.

   A. Texas Real Estate Commission
   B. Third party financing addendum
   C. Texas property tax exemptions
   D. None of the above

12. What is an ad valorem tax?

   A. Tax based on the assessed value of property
   B. Local taxes based on income
   C. Property taxes based on age
   D. Property taxes based on the number of dependents

13. How much errors and omissions insurance (E&O) does the state of Texas require a real estate broker to have?

    A. E&O is not required
    B. $500,000.00
    C. $1,000,000.00
    D. $750,000.00

14. When should a buyer have the survey pulled and get a title insurance property by the seller?

    A. Prior to the execution of the purchase and sale contract
    B. The buyer does not need to do either
    C. Within 20 days of the execution of the purchase and sale contract
    D. Within 10 days of the execution of the purchase and sale contract

15. Which is **not** a layer of the Texas survey system?

    A. Texas RRC district layer
    B. Texas bay tracts layer
    C. Texas coast layer
    D. Texas land survey layer

16. Which contract is used for the resale of residential properties?

    A. Residential condominium contract
    B. One to four family residential contract
    C. New home contract (completed construction)
    D. Unimproved property contract

17. A licensee must notify the sponsoring broker and _____ within 30 days when a licensee decides to perform real estate business by another name.

    A.   Any future clients
    B.   A lending company
    C.   They do not need to tell anyone
    D.   TREC

18. Texas Property Code requires homeowners who want to sell their property to fill out a _____.

    A.   Fitness determination form
    B.   Background history form
    C.   Seller's disclosure form
    D.   Public information request form

19. Who is **not** required to be licensed to sell real estate?

    A.   Real estate broker owners
    B.   Out of state real estate agents
    C.   State of Texas auctioneers
    D.   None of the above

20. Texas law does **not** allow agents to be a _____, which is when an agent represents both parties.

    A.   Dual agent
    B.   Subagent
    C.   General agent
    D.   Special agent

21. What is the purpose of the Texas Real Estate Licensing Act (TRELA)?

    A.   Establish rules that licensees need to follow in order to obtain and maintain a license

    B.   List of penalties for violations of the license act

    C.   Protect brokers from unfair activities by competitors

    D.   All of the above

22. A realtor advertisement in the local paper must include all of the following except _____.

    A.   The name of the broker

    B.   The name of the firm, if it is registered with TREC

    C.   Phone number, email address and fax number

    D.   The name of the seller

23. What is the Real Estate Recovery Trust Account and Fund?

    A.   A real estate recovery fund used to reimburse consumers who suffer damages caused by TREC license holders

    B.   A recovery fund funded by the federal government

    C.   A trust account to reimburse license holders who suffer damages caused by clients

    D.   A fund to reimburse property holders due to natural disasters

24. What is the statute of limitations for a breach of contract in Texas?

    A.   2 years

    B.   3 years

    C.   4 years

    D.   5 years

25. If a real estate trust account collects interest, the interest Is kept by?

A. The broker or the principal
B. The broker only
C. The principal only
D. TREC

26. The final signature on a purchase and sales agreement is the _____.

A. Buyer
B. Licensed agent
C. Seller
D. Lender

27. When was the Texas Real Estate Commission created?

A. 1968
B. 1980
C. 1949
D. 1965

28. What happens if a licensee does not respond to a subpoena?

A. The Attorney General can enforce the subpoena
B. The licensee does not need to respond to the subpoena
C. The licensee can be fired from their job
D. None of the above

29. The _____ drafts and advises TREC contracts and consists of 13 members.

    A. Texas Real Estate Licensing Act
    B. Texas Broker Committee
    C. Information About Brokerage Services
    D. Real Estate Broker-Lawyer Committee

30. Where does TREC hold hearings?

    A. TREC headquarters
    B. Local courthouse
    C. State courthouse
    D. At the real estate agent's office

31. The state of Texas does not have a _____. Which states a home cannot be redeemed once it has been foreclosed?

    A. Statutory right of redemption
    B. Power of sale clause
    C. Forbearance
    D. Loan modification

32. Which cannot be deducted from a property owner's personal home for tax purposes?

    A. Interest paid
    B. Property taxes paid
    C. Depreciation
    D. Itemized expenditures

33. _____ states that when the words "grant" or "convey" are used in a deed, the seller promises the property is free from encumbrances.

    A. Texas Real Estate Commission
    B. Texas Property Code
    C. Texas Real Estate Licensing Act
    D. General warranty deed

34. Which type of deed is used in transferring property in the state of Texas?

    A. General warranty deed
    B. Special warranty deed
    C. Quitclaim deed
    D. All of the above

35. _____ are regulations that govern the design, maintenance, construction and alteration of structures.

    A. Building codes
    B. Homeowner's association
    C. Appraisal
    D. Option period

36. A one to four family residential contract is not used for the resale of which type of property?

    A. Condominiums
    B. Tri-plex
    C. Single family home
    D. Four-plex

37. _____ are a form of private controls on land use.

   A. Security deposits
   B. Restrictive covenants
   C. Intermediaries
   D. Tenancy in common

38. Which statement is true about eviction?

   A. A landlord must legally terminate the tenancy prior to evicting a tenant
   B. A landlord needs to file an eviction lawsuit if the tenant does not move out after receiving a written notice
   C. A tenant can decide to fight an eviction
   D. All of the above

39. Which is an example of a latent defect?

   A. Worn carpet
   B. Chipped paint
   C. Foundation instabilities
   D. Cracked window

40. What is the statute of limitations for the Texas Deceptive Trade Practices Act?

   A. 5 years
   B. 1 year
   C. 2 years
   D. 10 years

THIS IS THE END OF THE STATE PORTION.

Answer Key – National Portion

1.	A	21.	A	41.	C	61.	D	81.	B
2.	B	22.	A	42.	B	62.	D	82.	D
3.	B	23.	B	43.	A	63.	C	83.	A
4.	A	24.	D	44.	D	64.	A	84.	B
5.	D	25.	C	45.	A	65.	A	85.	C
6.	B	26.	C	46.	C	66.	C		
7.	C	27.	C	47.	D	67.	B		
8.	D	28.	A	48.	B	68.	B		
9.	A	29.	D	49.	C	69.	A		
10.	B	30.	B	50.	A	70.	C		
11.	B	31.	D	51.	B	71.	D		
12.	A	32.	A	52.	B	72.	D		
13.	A	33.	A	53.	B	73.	A		
14.	C	34.	D	54.	D	74.	A		
15.	D	35.	A	55.	A	75.	D		
16.	A	36.	A	56.	C	76.	A		
17.	B	37.	D	57.	A	77.	A		
18.	C	38.	B	58.	A	78.	A		
19.	C	39.	B	59.	B	79.	B		
20.	D	40.	D	60.	C	80.	A		

1. **A) A loan that has a predetermined repayment interest rate**

Commonly compared to floating rate, which is a loan that uses external factors as a benchmark for interest rates and is usually fluctuating based on the external market.

2. **B) Civil Rights Act of 1866**

This act declares all citizens equal and under the protection of the law. The law emphasized protecting all citizens of African descent during the Civil War.

3. **B) Promissory note**

This is a financial document by the issuer to the payee that contains a promise to make payment for a definite sum of money. It is usually valid for payment either on demand or on a specified date. It usually contains information regarding the principal amount, interest rate, date and place of issuance, maturity date and signature of the parties involved.

4.   **A) Refinancing**

This is the process of replacing an existing mortgage with another that offers more favorable terms to the borrower. Refinancing enables a borrower to negotiate for lower monthly payments, lower interest rates and renegotiate the loan payment term.

5.   **D) All of the above**

An appurtenance is real property fixed to the land that is passed along with the sale of a property.

6.   **B) Certificate of deposit**

This is a product offered by banks and credit facilities to customers enabling them to deposit a lump sum amount for a predetermined period with an agreed upon interest rate premium. Doing some research on the certificate of deposit terms offered by the different available facilities is important to yield better returns.

7.   **C) $250,000**

$225,000 / (1 - 0.1) = $250,000

8.   **D) Annual percentage rate**

This is the annual rate charged on a loan or investment. It is usually used to express the actual annual cost of funds over the lifespan of a loan or cash investment. As loan arrangements vary among institutions and the situation surrounding the loan, a standardized APR is set to protect borrowers from unreasonably high interest rates.

9.   **A) Public auctions**

Homes are usually put on auction due to default on a mortgage or property taxes. Buying a house at an auction is risky as it often does not give the buyer a chance to view the interior of the house. When buying a property at an auction, it is necessary to run background research on the property.

10.   **B) Pre-qualification**

These is the process of reviewing clients' creditworthiness and is usually used as a marketing strategy to obtain new clients. Creditors usually mail a potential borrower outlining maximum limit for loan.

11. **B) Power of attorney**

This is a legal document that transfers rights to act in place of a principal in the event that they are unable to act for themselves. The terms of the contract usually include what can be managed and where the power of the agent ends.

12. **A) Exclusive listing**

An exclusive listing is an agreement between a seller and an agent stating that commission on a sale can only be earned when a sale is made within a specified period of time. The timeframe for the sale is usually agreed on by both parties while entering the agreement.

13. **A) Single agency**

This is brokerage agreement where a buying agent is assigned the role to represent a buyer and works in single agency capacity as the buyer's agent. This agent is bound by fiduciary duties to the buyer and cannot disclose any confidential information to the other party.

14. **C) Arms-length transaction**

This is a transaction where both the buyer and the seller are acting in self-interest with an aim of getting the better deal. The discrepancy is usually solved when both parties agree on a middle ground that fulfills the interests of both the buyer and the seller.

15. **D) Adjustment date**

This is the changing of a date where calculations on items such as property taxes, rent and damage deposits are done.

16. **A) Assumable mortgage**

This is a mortgage arrangement that allows the seller to transfer the terms and conditions of a mortgage to a buyer. In this case, a buyer absorbs the seller's remaining debt instead of taking out a new mortgage.

17. **B) Call option**

This is a contract signed by both the buyer and the seller giving one party the right to sell and the other the right to buy a property on a future date. The price of the property is usually included in the contract and remains the same regardless of inflation or market shifts.

18. **C) A specified expiration date**

An exclusive listing contract is an agreement where a real estate agent receives commission within a specified amount of time. The agent receives commission no matter how the buyer is found.

19. **C) Reciprocity**

Real estate license reciprocity allows agents to obtain a real estate license in another state by taking the reciprocal state's exam.

20. **D) Privacy**

The 6 fiduciary duties of a real estate agent are: **O**bedience, **L**oyalty, **D**isclosure, **C**onfidentiality, **A**ccountability, and **R**easonable care / diligence (OLDCAR)

21. **A) Conditions that must be met by both the buyer and the seller before closing**

They are set in place to protect the parties involved in the contract. A breach in the contingencies results in the immediate termination of the contract.

22. **A) Any individual whose name appears on the loan document**

This is often someone whose credit score was taken into consideration when determining whether or not a loan can be extended. A co-borrower can be beneficial for a borrower that is unable to get favorable interest rates.

23. **B) Construction loan**

This is a short-term loan that is usually taken to finance the construction of a home or real estate property. It is usually taken to provide cash flow before larger funding is approved.

24. **D) Final walkthrough**

This is a visit done to the property by the buyer after all financing has been secured. A buyer is required to visit the premise and establish whether all the things that were discussed in the contract have been met prior to closing the deal.

25. **C) Fixed mortgage rate**

This is a mortgage loan whose interest rate remains the same throughout the longevity of the loan.

26. **C) Loan to value ratio**

This is defined as the percentage of the home's value owned by the borrower after making a down payment. It is calculated by taking the mortgage loan amount and dividing it by the appraisal value of the property being bought. The higher the loan to value ratio, the less likely lenders are to agree to loans.

27. **C) 20%**

($1,000 * 12) / $60,000 = 0.2

28. **A) Vicarious liability**

This is a secondary form of liability where a superior is held accountable for the actions of his subordinates. In the real estate sector, vicarious liability arises when an agent hired by either the buyer or seller acts inappropriately. In this case, the client is held accountable for the misconduct of his agent.

29. **D) Agency disclosure statement**

This is a statement signed by both the seller and buyer prior to the real estate transaction. Its role is to disclose the role of the agent in the transaction. An agent can either be a broker for either the buyer or the seller, a dual agent or a sub agent. In order to enforce disclosure laws, some states have a disclosure form written into law.

30. **B) Price fixing**

This is a situation that arises where a number of real estate agencies that dominate the market agree on a set commission. Brokers are required by law to set their individual commissions where consideration to the market going rate is allowed. Choosing to agree on a set standard commission could result in the suspension of a broker's license. These laws were set in place to protect the buyers and sellers in the market.

31. **D) IRS**

The IRS uses the general rule that an individual can be classified as an independent contractor if the payer has the right to control the result of work and not how it will be done.

32. **A) Freehold**

Freehold title is a title given to a freehold property where the owner owns the unit and the land on which the establishment has been developed and anything that is erected on the land.

33. **A) $0**

According to the Taxpayer Relief Act of 1997, a married couple is eligible for exemption from capital gain tax on profits of up to $500,000. This can only be claimed provided the property is the primary home of the selling couple meaning they have been living there for at least 2 years. Therefore, Mr. and Mrs. Smith do not owe anything in capital gain tax.

34. **D) Suspended**

He can choose to wait for the suspension to be lifted or look for another broker. A license can be suspended due to violation of insurance laws, providing materially misleading information and fraudulent practices. A revoked can only be reinstated after one year with undeniable evidence of trustworthiness and ability to uphold the law.

35. **A) Umbrella policy**

An umbrella insurance policy is an excess liability policy that is often used as a fail-safe for assets and savings. It is mostly used by people that are at risk of being sued. Contrary to popular belief, an umbrella policy does not cover additional risk area but acts as an addition to an already existing insurance.

36. **A) Comparative Market Analysis**

Comparative Market Analysis is never used in valuation as it is based on the market value of similar properties whereas no two real properties are alike.

37. **D) Voidable Contract**

A voidable contract is a formal agreement between parties that can be rendered obsolete due to legal factors. Some of the factors that can result in a voidable contract being rejected are fraud, undisclosed facts and a breach of the contract. A voidable contract is always considered legal unless rendered unenforceable.

38. **B) Disclosure**

Fiduciary duties arise when an agency operates on behalf of a client. In this case the agent is legally mandated to act in the best interest of the client. When an agent fails to disclose facts that may influence the final decision of the client, he is in violation of the disclosure clause.

39. **B) Joint tenancy**

A joint tenancy is an arrangement where two or more parties agree to co-own a property with equal rights and obligations. Upon death of a partner, the property remains solely in the ownership of the surviving partner. A joint tenancy has to be entered at the same time through a deed. Joint tenancy has the advantage of avoiding legal battles after the demise of a partner but can be hard to settle in the event of a divorced couple.

40. **D) Proprietary lease**

A proprietary lease is a is an agreement that allows a shareholder in a housing corporation to live in a unit equaling their stakes in the corporation. A shareholder does not buy the property but shares in the corporation. In this case, the shares act as collateral on the lease.

41. **C) Void**

This means to be obsolete and have no enforceable terms. Parties to a void contract are not bound by its terms making the contract unenforceable.

42. **B) 43,560**

An acre is a standard unit for measuring land. An acre does not have to be square shaped but contains an equivalent of 43560 square feet.

43. **A) 100 amps**

The minimum is 100 amps as anything below that may not be able to sustain the electric needs of a home. Larger homes can have between 150 and 200 amps based on the type of electronic systems installed. Having a proper electrical distribution in the home will also avoid trips.

44. **D) 75%**

750,000 / 1,000,000 = 0.75

The debt-to-equity ratio is used to determine whether a buyer can afford a house or to refinance an already owned property.

45. **A) FEMA**

The Federal Emergency Management Agency focuses on promoting the need to work together to support citizens and fast respondents. Its goal is to ensure citizens build and sustain to prepare for and recover from calamities.

46. **C) Blueprint**

A blueprint is a reproduction of a technical drawing on a light sensitive sheet that is done using a contact printer. A blueprint is usually required to predetermine the design and pattern that is going to be followed in a construction.

47. **D) UFFI**

Urea Formaldehyde Foam Insulation was used for house insulation in the 70s due to its high thermal resistance. Testing in the lab showed that the insulation produced fumes that were toxic for humans and the environment leading to its ban in 1982.

48. **B) Dual agency**

Dual agency is legal in Pennsylvania provided both the buyer and the seller agree to the arrangement after pros and cons of the relationship are laid on the table. Opting to have a dual agent means that the client cannot expect the agent to act in their best interest as he is representing two conflicting interests.

49. **C) Fixed mortgage rate**

This is an agreement between the seller and agent conveying that the agent is eligible for commission on the sale of the property regardless of who found the buyer. The terms of the agreement are only valid for a sale made within the time period of the agreement.

50. **A) The equipment is considered trade fixtures**

Trade fixtures are removable personal property that are installed in a leased space to facilitate business running. For one to be allowed to remove a fixture, it must be essential for the running of the business to not cause damage to the property and be removed before the expiry of the lease.

51. **B) Easement in gross**

The rights associated by the easement are irrevocable for the person granted. A transfer of the property to another individual through sale or inheritance does not warrant an automatic transfer of the rights to the new owner. This renders the easement of gross void.

52. **B) Shingles**

These are a covering for pitched roofs and are laid in an overlapping style. Shingles are made in a number of shapes and materials. They are used mainly for decorative purposes. In some cases, they are put in place to provide protection from the effects of rain, hail and snow.

53. **B) Seller and broker**

The seller and broker are usually responsible for agreeing in the amount of commission that should be paid to the broker

54. **D) Statute of limitations**

The statute of limitations is a law that sets the maximum period of time parties involved in a rift have to initiate legal proceedings from the day of the occurrence of the event. The time allocated to offences differs according to the nature of the offence.

55. **A) Mortgagor**

A mortgagor is an individual that borrows money from a lender in order to purchase a property. The lending is based on the individual's credit score and collateral. A title must be handed to the lender as collateral for the loan.

56.   **C) Percentage lease**

A percentage lease is a type of lease where the tenant pays rent plus a percentage of any revenue earned while doing business on the property. This agreement significantly reduces the rent paid. The parties involved agree on a base point where percentage lease kicks in.

57.   **A) It protected against racial discrimination**

The Civil Rights act of 1866 banned racial discrimination in real estate and housing transactions. People of any race had equal rights as whites to buy, sell, or lease property.

58.   **A) It required agencies to publicize records to the Federal Register**

The Privacy Act of 1974 is an act that established code of fair information maintenance governing the collection, use and maintenance of individuals that is maintained by federal agencies. The act required the agencies to publicize the records in the Federal Register.

59.   **B) It granted reparations to Japanese Americans interned by the government during World War II**

The Civil Liberties Act of 1988 granted the Japanese Americans that has been interned by the government during World War 2 reparation.

60.   **C) Blockbusting**

This is the act of trying to manipulate tenants to sell or rent their properties at lower rates due to an influx of minority groups in a once segregated neighborhood.

61.   **D) Qualified fee estate**

This is an estate agreement that facilitates the grantor to propose a set of conditions. A breach in the condition limitation may result in termination of the agreement. A quality fee estate can also be based on the occurrence of a predetermined event.

62.   **D) Refusal of a lending institution to make a loan because the area is integrated or populated by culturally diverse people**

This usually occurs when a lending institution has a map of areas they would not like to initiate credit in. Potential property owners are denied mortgages despite great credit scores due to the location of the property they intend to purchase.

63.   **C) Tenancy by entirety**

Only married couples can enter this type of co-ownership where the property is jointly owned as a single entity. It facilitates right of survivorship and can be terminated upon death of spouse or divorce.

64.   **A) Escheat**

A property can be reverted to the state if no claimants have come forth to claim the property or the available heir has been deemed legally unfit to be granted ownership. It is revocable once a legal heir claims the property.

65.   **A) $1,000**

($150,000 * 0.08) / 12 = $1,000

66.   **C) Acceleration clause**

This is a contract that allows a lender to require full settlement of an outstanding loan due to a breach of predetermined conditions.

67.   **B) Graduated mortgage**

This is a fixed price loan that allows the borrower to make smaller payments on the loan in the earlier payment years and continues to increase gradually until the mortgage is paid off. It considers individuals who were otherwise not qualified for the higher rate to qualify.

68.   **B) Blanket mortgage**

A blanket mortgage is a mortgage that covers two or more pieces of real estate. The real estate property is held as collateral. Individual properties can be sold without having to retire the mortgage. This insurance is usually taken when purchasing and developing land.

69.   **A) Both offers**

The agent is required by fiduciary duties to present both the offers to the client. Choosing to present the higher offer to the client in order to reap higher commission from the sale is a breach of fiduciary duties.

70.   **C) Purchase money**

This is a mortgage issued by the seller as part of a real estate transaction. This arrangement is usually reached when the buyer is not eligible for the traditional mortgage. A down payment is usually placed on the property as an order of the financial transaction.

71.   **D) Appraisal**

An appraisal is an opinion usually given by a professional on the market value of a property. Properties usually require an appraisal is unique and market value of similar properties may not offer an accurate value of the property.

72. **D) Lead**

Lead is a periodic metal that was used in paint in the 1970s as it accelerated drying, maintained a fresh appearance and resisted moisture. Older plumbing systems used lead lines and water often corroded the material as it was transported to the consumer's taps. Use of lead in paint was discontinued as it was found to cause nervous system damage and stunted growth in children.

73. **A) Rentable square footage**

Rentable square footage is inclusive of the usable square footage and common areas. The price per rentable square foot is usually calculated using a pro-rata calculation based on the size of the space being leased.

74. **A) CFCs**

CFCs are nonflammable chemicals that are commonly used in aerosol sprays and industrial cleaning products. Once these chemicals are released into the atmosphere they rise into the stratosphere where ultraviolet rays from the sun break them down. This breakdown releases chlorine atoms that destroy ozone molecules therefore forming ozone holes.

75. **D) All of the above**

Liability insurance covers everything from house fires, injuries incurred on the property, floods, injured domestic workers, falling trees, and more.

76. **A) To transfer title rights**

The buyer and seller must both sign a deed to transfer the property's ownership.

77. **A) Absorption rate**

This is a ration of the number of properties that have been sold against the number of properties that are available for sale within a specified area.

78. **A) Fiduciary**

Fiduciary is the relationship between client and broker. An agent is the fiduciary of the client.

79. **B) A set of laws that apply to a person who acts on behalf of another person**

The law of agency is a set of duties that real estate professionals owe to their clients, including disclosures that must be made to the client. These duties are set by each state.

80. **A) Real property that is converted into personal property**

There are two types of severance, actual severance and constructive severance. An actual severance is when an item is removed from the land and a constructive severance is when an item is detached by intent.

81.   **B) Plottage**

Plottage occurs when the total value of a combined parcel is worth more than the sum of the individual parcels. The process of combining the parcel is called assemblage.

82.   **D) A list of prospects who have inquired or visited the property**

A traffic report keeps a count of prospective buyers who have called about or visited the property.

83.   **A) Provide buyers and sellers with disclosures regarding settlement costs**

RESPA is a consumer protection act that provides procedures that need to be followed in one-to-four residential real estate sales. It assists in eliminating abusive practices during settlements, bars kickback and limits the use of escrow accounts

84.   **B) Blockbusting**

An illegal act that is not permitted by the Fair Housing Laws. This method manipulates homeowners into selling or renting their home at a lower price by falsely stating that minorities (racial, religious, etc.,) are moving into a once segregated neighborhood.

85.   **C) Partially amortized loan**

A property manager is responsible for maintaining a client's property and maximizing the return on the client's investment. When a licensee acts on behalf of a client and doing the above, they are acting as a property manager.

Answer Key – State Portion

1.	A	21.	D
2.	C	22.	D
3.	D	23.	A
4.	B	24.	C
5.	C	25.	A
6.	A	26.	C
7.	D	27.	C
8.	B	28.	A
9.	C	29.	D
10.	A	30.	A
11.	B	31.	A
12.	A	32.	C
13.	A	33.	B
14.	C	34.	D
15.	C	35.	A
16.	B	36.	A
17.	D	37.	B
18.	C	38.	D
19.	C	39.	C
20.	A	40.	C

1. **A) 9**

There are 9 members on the Texas Real Estate commission. 6 are real estate brokers and 3 are members of the public.

2. **C) Disclose, in writing, their intent to sell their own property**

When the principal has a real estate license, they must disclose their license in the contract, lease or other form of writing prior to an agreement being signed. A disclosure is required even if the license is inactive.

3. **D) A salesperson cannot pay an unlicensed customer**

The licensed salesperson cannot give cash to an unlicensed customer. They can, however, give a non-cash gift who $50 or less and not violate TREC and TRELA rules.

4.   **B) Municipal utility district**

MUD is authorized by TREC to provided water, sewage, drainage and other utility related services. A MUD is created when property owners in the proposed district petition the Texas Commission of Environmental Quality.

5.   **C) 2 business days**

TREC requires earnest money to be deposited within 2 business days of receiving the money.

6.   **A) The option period is negotiable**

The option period is negotiable but is anywhere between 1 and 10 days. The option period begins the day after the effective day of contract. I.e. A contract is executed on May 2nd, option period begins May 3rd.

7.   **D) All of the above**

Up to one year of jail time and a fine can be administrated as well as an administrative penalty from TREC of up to $5,000.00. TREC can also issue a cease and desist order and can obtain injunctive relief if a civil court case is pursued.

8.   **B) 4 years**

A broker needs to keep documents for a minimum of 4 years according to Texas law. The time frame begins 4 years from the date of closing or termination of a contract and need to be readily made available to the commission.

9.   **C) 200 acres**

Texas allows a family to have 200 acres of rural homesteads, and 100 acres for a single adult, including property improvements. In urban areas the limit is 10 acres including property improvements.

10.   **A) 18 hours**

A broker needs to complete 18 hours of continuing education. 8 of those hours are TREC legal updates I and II and 10 hours are elective continuing education.

11.   **B) Third party financing addendum**

This addendum is not required to be put into a contract but if the lender determines that the appraisal of the property does not satisfy the lender's underwriting requirements i.e. the appraisal is too low, then the contract can be terminated.

12. **A) Tax based on the assessed value of property**

This tax is locally assessed, and the county appraisal district appraises the property. The local taxing units set the rates and collect the tax. In Texas, property taxes are a large source of assistance to public schools, playgrounds, libraries and other services.

13. **A) E&O is not required**

While E&O is not required, many clients may require proof of this insurance. It provides crucial protection to brokers and is required in some states.

14. **C) Within 20 days of the execution of the purchase and sale contract**

Prior to 20 days after the title company receives a copy of the contract a seller needs to provide the buyer the survey and commitment for title insurance.

15. **C) Texas coast layer**

The three layers are the Texas RRC district layer which contains the geographic boundaries for the 12 railroad districts, the Texas bay tracts layer represents the survey areas present in bays along the east coast and the Texas land survey layer which splits the state into areas which comprise of tracts, sections and labors.

16. **B) One to four family residential**

The most frequently used contract form, it is used for the sale of single, family home, duplex, tri-plex or four-plex residential properties. This contract cannot be used for new homes sold by a builder, condominium or farm and ranch properties.

17. **D) TREC**

A licensee must inform the Texas Real Estate Commission when they change their name within 30 days of the name change.

18. **C) Seller's disclosure form**

Sellers must fill out this form and disclose any issues with the property that they are aware of. They must also provide a historical account of the home.

19. **C) State of Texas auctioneers**

Auctioneers do not need a real estate license to auction off real estate property. A license is required to become an auctioneer.

20. **A) Dual agent**

A dual agency is not permitted in the state of Texas. The broker can act as an intermediary. If this occurs in errors, the broker must resolve this by acting as an intermediary or only representing one of the principals.

21. **D) All of the above**

The TRELA ensures high standards of ethics and practice in the Texas real estate industry. It is important for an agent and broker to understand the TRELA.

22. **D) The name of the seller**

The name of the seller is not required in real estate advertisement and the advertisement cannot be misleading. For example, using an "owner" title can be misleading because it implies the sales agent is the owner of the brokerage.

23. **A) A real estate fund used to reimburse consumers who suffer damages caused by TREC license holders**

This is one of two real estate recovery funds in Texas. Consumers can file an application for payment from this fund after they file a suit and obtain a judgement in civil court for damages caused by a licensed broker, agent or easement agent.

24. **C) 4 years**

This statute of limitations applies to contractual obligations including certain transfers of real property and fiduciary duty claims.

25. **A) The broker or the principal**

The broker can keep the interest if the principal has a signed agreement authorizing the broker to keep the interest. If the principal does not agree to the above terms, then the interest must be treated in the same manner as the deposited money.

26. **C) Seller**

The seller is the final signee of the purchase and sales agreement.

27. **C) 1949**

The Texas Legislature established TREC in 1949. It also shares resources with the TALCB.

28. **A) The Attorney General can enforce the subpoena**

TREC has the power to file a suit with the Attorney General to enforce the subpoena. This is called the subpoena power held by TREC.

29. **D) Real Estate Broker-Lawyer Committee**

This committee is responsible for drafting and advising TREC contracts. It consists of 13 members 6 of whom are appointed by the commission, another 6 appointed by the president of the state bar of Texas and 1 appointed by the governor.

30. **A) TREC headquarters**

The hearings are held at TREC headquarters in Austin, Texas unless the licensee asks for the hearing to be held in their county.

31. **A) Statutory right of redemption**

Texas allows a property to be redeem prior to a foreclosure sale but does not allow this after the foreclosed home has been sold. The statutory right of redemption allows borrowers to reclaim property after a sale by paying the foreclosure sale price or the full amount owed to the bank and any additional charges.

32. **C) Depreciation**

Depreciation cannot be deducted from a property owner's personal home for tax purposes. Property taxes paid, interest paid, and itemized expenditures can be deducted.

33. **B) Texas Property Code**

The code also states that a grantor has not transferred any part of the property to anyone else if the words "grant" or "convey" are used in a deed.

34. **D) All of the above**

These are all types of deeds used to transfer property in Texas. General warranty deeds are the most common and quitclaim deeds and are discouraged.

35. **A) Building codes**

Building codes specify requirement to ensure the safeguard of building occupants. They address health, safety, and welfare issues. The state of Texas does not have specified residential building codes but have adopted international codes.

36. **A) Condominium**

Sales involving condominiums, new homes being sold by a builder, and farm and ranch properties cannot use the one to four family residential contract.

37. **B) Restrictive covenants**

This type of covenant specifies how a property can be used in Texas. I.e. a deed can state that a specific piece of land can be used for single-family residences only.

38. **D) All of the above**

Texas law requires a landlord to submit an eviction lawsuit if a tenant does not move out after receiving a termination letter. A landlord has the right to fight the eviction and the most common defense is that the landlord did not follow the rules of eviction.

39. **C) Foundation instabilities**

Latent defects are faults that could not have been discovered by a reasonably thorough inspection prior to the sale. Leaks in the ceiling and other toxic conditions are considered latent defects.

40. **C) 2 years**

The lawsuit must be filed within two years after the date on which the deceptive act occurred. If the act took place over time, then it is within two years of the date of the first action.

Practice Test 2

Directions:

1. You have a 150-minute time limit for the national portion, and a 90-minute time limit for the state portion.

2. To pass, you must answer at least 56 out of 85 questions correctly on the national portion **AND** at least 21 out of 40 questions on the state portion.

3. Some questions will require mathematics. You may use a calculator.

4. **Phones and pagers are not allowed. Having either will result in automatic dismissal from the exam and nullification of exam scores.**

Tips:

-   Answer all questions even if you are unsure.
-   Mark any questions you are stuck on and revisit them after you are done. The exam is timed so make sure you finish as many questions as you can.
-   After reading the question, try answering it in your head first to avoid getting confused by the choices.
-   Read the entire question before looking at the answers.
-   Use the process of elimination to filter out choices that don't seem correct to increase your chances of selecting the correct answer.
-   Be aware of important keywords like **not, sometimes, always,** and **never**. These words completely alter the ask of the question so it's important to keep track of them.

PLEASE READ THESE INSTRUCTIONS CAREFULLY.

Name: _____   Date: _____

NATIONAL PORTION

1.	Ⓐ Ⓑ Ⓒ Ⓓ	31.	Ⓐ Ⓑ Ⓒ Ⓓ	61.	Ⓐ Ⓑ Ⓒ Ⓓ
2.	Ⓐ Ⓑ Ⓒ Ⓓ	32.	Ⓐ Ⓑ Ⓒ Ⓓ	62.	Ⓐ Ⓑ Ⓒ Ⓓ
3.	Ⓐ Ⓑ Ⓒ Ⓓ	33.	Ⓐ Ⓑ Ⓒ Ⓓ	63.	Ⓐ Ⓑ Ⓒ Ⓓ
4.	Ⓐ Ⓑ Ⓒ Ⓓ	34.	Ⓐ Ⓑ Ⓒ Ⓓ	64.	Ⓐ Ⓑ Ⓒ Ⓓ
5.	Ⓐ Ⓑ Ⓒ Ⓓ	35.	Ⓐ Ⓑ Ⓒ Ⓓ	65.	Ⓐ Ⓑ Ⓒ Ⓓ
6.	Ⓐ Ⓑ Ⓒ Ⓓ	36.	Ⓐ Ⓑ Ⓒ Ⓓ	66.	Ⓐ Ⓑ Ⓒ Ⓓ
7.	Ⓐ Ⓑ Ⓒ Ⓓ	37.	Ⓐ Ⓑ Ⓒ Ⓓ	67.	Ⓐ Ⓑ Ⓒ Ⓓ
8.	Ⓐ Ⓑ Ⓒ Ⓓ	38.	Ⓐ Ⓑ Ⓒ Ⓓ	68.	Ⓐ Ⓑ Ⓒ Ⓓ
9.	Ⓐ Ⓑ Ⓒ Ⓓ	39.	Ⓐ Ⓑ Ⓒ Ⓓ	69.	Ⓐ Ⓑ Ⓒ Ⓓ
10.	Ⓐ Ⓑ Ⓒ Ⓓ	40.	Ⓐ Ⓑ Ⓒ Ⓓ	70.	Ⓐ Ⓑ Ⓒ Ⓓ
11.	Ⓐ Ⓑ Ⓒ Ⓓ	41.	Ⓐ Ⓑ Ⓒ Ⓓ	71.	Ⓐ Ⓑ Ⓒ Ⓓ
12.	Ⓐ Ⓑ Ⓒ Ⓓ	42.	Ⓐ Ⓑ Ⓒ Ⓓ	72.	Ⓐ Ⓑ Ⓒ Ⓓ
13.	Ⓐ Ⓑ Ⓒ Ⓓ	43.	Ⓐ Ⓑ Ⓒ Ⓓ	73.	Ⓐ Ⓑ Ⓒ Ⓓ
14.	Ⓐ Ⓑ Ⓒ Ⓓ	44.	Ⓐ Ⓑ Ⓒ Ⓓ	74.	Ⓐ Ⓑ Ⓒ Ⓓ
15.	Ⓐ Ⓑ Ⓒ Ⓓ	45.	Ⓐ Ⓑ Ⓒ Ⓓ	75.	Ⓐ Ⓑ Ⓒ Ⓓ
16.	Ⓐ Ⓑ Ⓒ Ⓓ	46.	Ⓐ Ⓑ Ⓒ Ⓓ	76.	Ⓐ Ⓑ Ⓒ Ⓓ
17	Ⓐ Ⓑ Ⓒ Ⓓ	47.	Ⓐ Ⓑ Ⓒ Ⓓ	77.	Ⓐ Ⓑ Ⓒ Ⓓ
18.	Ⓐ Ⓑ Ⓒ Ⓓ	48.	Ⓐ Ⓑ Ⓒ Ⓓ	78.	Ⓐ Ⓑ Ⓒ Ⓓ
19.	Ⓐ Ⓑ Ⓒ Ⓓ	49.	Ⓐ Ⓑ Ⓒ Ⓓ	79.	Ⓐ Ⓑ Ⓒ Ⓓ
20.	Ⓐ Ⓑ Ⓒ Ⓓ	50.	Ⓐ Ⓑ Ⓒ Ⓓ	80.	Ⓐ Ⓑ Ⓒ Ⓓ
21.	Ⓐ Ⓑ Ⓒ Ⓓ	51.	Ⓐ Ⓑ Ⓒ Ⓓ	81.	Ⓐ Ⓑ Ⓒ Ⓓ
22.	Ⓐ Ⓑ Ⓒ Ⓓ	52.	Ⓐ Ⓑ Ⓒ Ⓓ	82.	Ⓐ Ⓑ Ⓒ Ⓓ
23.	Ⓐ Ⓑ Ⓒ Ⓓ	53.	Ⓐ Ⓑ Ⓒ Ⓓ	83.	Ⓐ Ⓑ Ⓒ Ⓓ
24.	Ⓐ Ⓑ Ⓒ Ⓓ	54.	Ⓐ Ⓑ Ⓒ Ⓓ	84.	Ⓐ Ⓑ Ⓒ Ⓓ
25.	Ⓐ Ⓑ Ⓒ Ⓓ	55.	Ⓐ Ⓑ Ⓒ Ⓓ	85.	Ⓐ Ⓑ Ⓒ Ⓓ
26.	Ⓐ Ⓑ Ⓒ Ⓓ	56.	Ⓐ Ⓑ Ⓒ Ⓓ		
27.	Ⓐ Ⓑ Ⓒ Ⓓ	57.	Ⓐ Ⓑ Ⓒ Ⓓ		
28.	Ⓐ Ⓑ Ⓒ Ⓓ	58.	Ⓐ Ⓑ Ⓒ Ⓓ		
29.	Ⓐ Ⓑ Ⓒ Ⓓ	59.	Ⓐ Ⓑ Ⓒ Ⓓ		
30.	Ⓐ Ⓑ Ⓒ Ⓓ	60.	Ⓐ Ⓑ Ⓒ Ⓓ		

Name: _____   Date: _____

STATE PORTION

1.	Ⓐ Ⓑ Ⓒ Ⓓ	31.	Ⓐ Ⓑ Ⓒ Ⓓ
2.	Ⓐ Ⓑ Ⓒ Ⓓ	32.	Ⓐ Ⓑ Ⓒ Ⓓ
3.	Ⓐ Ⓑ Ⓒ Ⓓ	33.	Ⓐ Ⓑ Ⓒ Ⓓ
4.	Ⓐ Ⓑ Ⓒ Ⓓ	34.	Ⓐ Ⓑ Ⓒ Ⓓ
5.	Ⓐ Ⓑ Ⓒ Ⓓ	35.	Ⓐ Ⓑ Ⓒ Ⓓ
6.	Ⓐ Ⓑ Ⓒ Ⓓ	36.	Ⓐ Ⓑ Ⓒ Ⓓ
7.	Ⓐ Ⓑ Ⓒ Ⓓ	37.	Ⓐ Ⓑ Ⓒ Ⓓ
8.	Ⓐ Ⓑ Ⓒ Ⓓ	38.	Ⓐ Ⓑ Ⓒ Ⓓ
9.	Ⓐ Ⓑ Ⓒ Ⓓ	39.	Ⓐ Ⓑ Ⓒ Ⓓ
10.	Ⓐ Ⓑ Ⓒ Ⓓ	40.	Ⓐ Ⓑ Ⓒ Ⓓ
11.	Ⓐ Ⓑ Ⓒ Ⓓ		
12.	Ⓐ Ⓑ Ⓒ Ⓓ		
13.	Ⓐ Ⓑ Ⓒ Ⓓ		
14.	Ⓐ Ⓑ Ⓒ Ⓓ		
15.	Ⓐ Ⓑ Ⓒ Ⓓ		
16.	Ⓐ Ⓑ Ⓒ Ⓓ		
17	Ⓐ Ⓑ Ⓒ Ⓓ		
18.	Ⓐ Ⓑ Ⓒ Ⓓ		
19.	Ⓐ Ⓑ Ⓒ Ⓓ		
20.	Ⓐ Ⓑ Ⓒ Ⓓ		
21.	Ⓐ Ⓑ Ⓒ Ⓓ		
22.	Ⓐ Ⓑ Ⓒ Ⓓ		
23.	Ⓐ Ⓑ Ⓒ Ⓓ		
24.	Ⓐ Ⓑ Ⓒ Ⓓ		
25.	Ⓐ Ⓑ Ⓒ Ⓓ		
26.	Ⓐ Ⓑ Ⓒ Ⓓ		
27.	Ⓐ Ⓑ Ⓒ Ⓓ		
28.	Ⓐ Ⓑ Ⓒ Ⓓ		
29.	Ⓐ Ⓑ Ⓒ Ⓓ		
30.	Ⓐ Ⓑ Ⓒ Ⓓ		

NATIONAL PORTION

1. What is the process of attempting to recover a loan from a borrower that has stopped making payments?

   A. Concession
   B. Final walk through
   C. Foreclosure
   D. Private mortgage insurance

2. What fibrous material causes cancer when released into the air?

   A. Asbestos
   B. Cotton
   C. Textiles
   D. Trunks

3. What are the vertical beams that frame the house?

   A. Frames
   B. Joists
   C. Shingles
   D. Studs

4. What is a reason a broker may be suspended or have their license revoked?

   A. Misrepresentation
   B. Failure to retain clients
   C. Failure to sell property within specified timeframe
   D. None of the above

5. A property manager makes routine rounds to repair air conditioning vents. What is the term used to refer to this?

   A. Aesthetic maintenance
   B. Avoiding depreciation
   C. Preventive maintenance
   D. Proration

6. What is another term that can be used to refer to the lender?

   A. Seller
   B. Mortgagee
   C. Mortgagor
   D. Loanee

7. If a seller nets $150,000 from the sale of her home, and the commission is 4%, how much did the home sell for?

   A. $144,000
   B. $148,500
   C. $156,000
   D. $156,250

8. What is the name given to the restriction of land usage by the local authorities?

   A. Building codes
   B. Denial
   C. Land zoning
   D. Property tax

9. What is the lender required to do once it is a borrower is unable to clear a mortgage?

   A. Threaten borrower
   B. Sell property without court order
   C. Initiate judicial foreclosure
   D. Evict the borrower

10. Which association represents title insurance?

   A. American Land Title Association
   B. CERCLA
   C. Fair Housing Act
   D. FEMA

11. Which law was passed to regulate credit bureaus?

   A. Annuity law
   B. Consumer credit law
   C. Fair Credit Reporting Act
   D. Truth in Lending Act

12. What is the legal right granted to exit a property?

   A. Easement
   B. Escheat
   C. Right of egress
   D. Right of ingress

13. What is the name given to non-monetary investment?

   A. Sweat equity
   B. Investment
   C. Capital
   D. Maintenance

14. What type of arrangement allows a borrower to negotiate a lower interest rate?

   A. Buydown
   B. Mortgage
   C. Purchase money
   D. Purchase price

15. What is a title without any lien?

   A. Clear title
   B. Deed
   C. Freehold
   D. Regular title

16. What is the name given to the breakdown of an individual's credit history?

   A. Credit assessment
   B. Credit report
   C. Financial record
   D. Repayment report

17. What is another term used to describe ownership?

A. Credit
B. Equity
C. Liability
D. Shares

18. What is the notice filed against a borrower on missing the repayment deadline?

A. Notice of cessation
B. Notice to cure
C. Notice of default
D. Notice of intention

19. What is the name given to describe the period a lender must keep a loan offer open to the borrower?

A. Due diligence period
B. Loan repayment period
C. Lock-in period
D. Target hold period

20. Which of the following is a lease break?

A. When a tenant breaks a rent prior to the date of expiry without a legal reason.
B. When a tenant terminates a contract once the lease has expired
C. When a tenant breaks a lease with the agreement of the landlord
D. When a landlord allows a tenant to sublease his residence

21. What is the term used to refer to a situation where the amount of funds required to meet an obligation are **not** available?

A. Buydown
B. Debt to income ratio
C. Escrow
D. Shortfall

22. What is the term used to describe a situation where taxes are reduced or completely scrapped to increase buyers in the market?

A. Tax abatement
B. Tax exemption
C. Tax evasion
D. Duty free

23. A property originally assessed at $500,000 appreciated at 4% the first year and then 5% the year after. What is its current value?

A. $525,000
B. $545,000
C. $546,000
D. None of the above

24. Which entity performs the percolation test?

A. Department of State
B. Building Inspector
C. Homeowners Association
D. Department of Health

25. If a property is taxed at 25% with a tax levy of $92,000, what is its assessed value?

    A. $65,000
    B. $115,000
    C. $122,666
    D. $368,000

26. What is the name given to a brief summary of the history of a title?

    A. Abstract of title
    B. Chain of title
    C. Deed chain
    D. History of deed

27. What material is used in construction to cover joints where two or more types of materials meet?

    A. Flashing
    B. Metal
    C. Wood
    D. Joint

28. What is the lowest section of the roof that overhangs beyond the sidewalls of the building?

    A. Eaves
    B. Joists
    C. Stud
    D. Shingles

29. Which real estate metric is found by dividing cash flow by the deposit and settlement costs?

    A. Cash out
    B. Cash on cash return
    C. Lock in period
    D. Loan to value ratio

30. Which board committee is responsible for maintaining the aesthetic view of a town?

    A. Architectural Review Board
    B. Federal government
    C. Municipality
    D. HOA

31. What type of lease is taken on a loft?

    A. Net lease
    B. Gross lease
    C. Percentage lease
    D. Proprietary lease

32. What clause can prohibit having loud parties?

    A. House rules
    B. Regulations
    C. Lease terms
    D. Noise permit

33. What is the measurement used to show the volatility of a market?

    A. Fluctuation rate
    B. Absorption rate
    C. Inflation
    D. Purchase deviation

34. What is the mortgage clause that allows a lender the right to demand immediate payment of a mortgage?

    A. Cancellation clause
    B. Acceleration clause
    C. Prepayment Penalty clause
    D. Release clause

35. Which agreement allows a property holder to cross another person's land?

    A. Easement appurtenant
    B. Easement in gross
    C. Prescriptive easement
    D. None of the above

36. Which of the following is insurance taken out as a protection against malfunctions associated with the acquisition of a new home?

    A. Flood insurance
    B. Homeowner's warranty insurance
    C. HO2
    D. Hazard insurance

37. What is it called when someone takes possession of a property without being the actual title holder?

    A. Acceleration clause
    B. Adverse possession
    C. Easement
    D. Escheat

38. What is a non-possessory interest in property or restrictive covenant burdening the title?

    A. Adverse possession
    B. Easement
    C. Encumbrance
    D. Escheat

39. What is the name given to the long beams that span the piers of a foundation offering support to the floor or ceiling?

    A. Eaves
    B. Frames
    C. Joists
    D. Studs

40. What conveys a grantor's interest in real property?

    A. Agreement
    B. Conveyance
    C. Offering the loan
    D. Title

41. What prohibits the solicitation of residential property listings?

    A. Commingling
    B. Non-solicitation order
    C. Regulation Z
    D. Termination of tenancy

42. What is exempt from property taxation?

    A. Colleges
    B. Office buildings
    C. Supermarkets
    D. Unoccupied land

43. Which fiduciary duty is violated by commingling?

    A. Accountability
    B. Disclosure
    C. Obedience
    D. Loyalty

44. What gives the government power to appropriate private property?

    A. Right of first refusal
    B. Riparian rights
    C. Eminent domain
    D. None of the above

45. What is the owner of a building prohibited to do regarding the disabled?

    A. Allow the disabled to be tenants
    B. Make the building accessible to the disabled
    C. Ensure they are treated like other tenants
    D. Refuse modifications for handicapped tenants

46. What act prohibits discrimination based on disability?

    A. The Americans with Disabilities Act of 1990
    B. Fair Housing Act
    C. Civil Rights Act of 1866
    D. Civil Right Act of 1964

47. What is the name given to a property tenure that can be terminated at any time?

    A. Tenancy in sufferance
    B. Terminated tenancy
    C. Tenancy in common
    D. Tenancy at will

48. If you have a loan of $350,000 with a 7% interest, how much do you pay in interest every month?

    A. $2,041
    B. $2,260
    C. $27,125
    D. $31,208

49. What law prohibits any type of discrimination on the basis of sex and gender?

A. Fair Housing Act
B. Civil Rights Act of 1866
C. Civil Rights Act Amendment of 1974
D. Americans with Disabilities Act

50. In 1988, the Civil Rights Act was amended to include?

A. Married women
B. Immigrants
C. Black people
D. Handicaps and familial status

51. What is the net income of a property valued at $500,000 and a capitalization rate of 14%?

A. $70,000
B. $43,000
C. $840,000
D. None of the above

52. What is the name of an appointed official who estimates the value of real property for taxing purposes?

A. Agent
B. Assessor
C. Appraiser
D. Tax official

53. What is the term used to describe a situation where a mortgage balance decreases due to periodic installments that pay down the principal and interest?

A. Adjustable-rate mortgage
B. Amortization
C. Lock-in period
D. Fixed-rate mortgage

54. What is an annual tax levied on the value of real property?

A. Capital gains tax
B. Real estate tax
C. Progressive tax
D. Regressive tax

55. What is the name given to a situation where an individual uses borrowed money to purchase a property?

A. Buydown
B. Purchase money
C. Leverage
D. Shorting

56. Which air conditioning system facilitates both heating and cooling?

A. Forced air system
B. Cooling system
C. Heating system
D. Thermostat

57. What is the waiting time for a real estate agent to renew a license once it is revoked?

- A. Two months
- B. One year
- C. Five years
- D. It is never reinstated

58. Who manages a co-op?

- A. Board of directors
- B. CEO
- C. Co-op developers
- D. Tenants

59. What is the value estimating process that uses similar available properties to determine the value of land?

- A. Mirror method
- B. Sales comparison method
- C. Allocation method
- D. Abstraction method

60. Who is required to sign a deed in a real estate transaction?

- A. Attorney
- B. Buyer
- C. Grantor
- D. Lender

61. What is a poisonous gas that comes from the breakdown of minerals in soil?

- A. Ammonia
- B. Chlorine
- C. Helium
- D. Radon

62. What are the rights of a person whose property is adjacent to or crossed by a river?

- A. Exclusive rights to sell
- B. Riparian rights
- C. Rights of first refusal
- D. Right of disclosure

63. What law requires full disclosure of all credit terms for consumer loans under the Truth in Lending Act?

- A. Americans with Disabilities Act
- B. Civil Rights Act
- C. Fair Housing Act
- D. Regulation Z

64. What is the name given to granting priority to an individual to buy or lease a property?

- A. Bundle of rights
- B. Exclusive right to sell
- C. Right of first refusal
- D. Right of possession

65. What is the loss of property value caused by economic or functional factors?

   A.   Economic obsolescence
   B.   Depreciation
   C.   Legal obsolescence
   D.   Aesthetic obsolescence

66. What kind of agent is a real estate agent?

   A.   Special agent
   B.   General agent
   C.   Dual agent
   D.   Subagent

67. What valuing method is Comparative Market Analysis **not** considered as?

   A.   Appraisal
   B.   Home valuing
   C.   Depreciation valuing
   D.   Tax returns valuing

68. What is a specific lien claimed by someone who has performed construction / repair / renovation work on the property and has **not** been paid?

   A.   Mechanic's lien
   B.   Involuntary lien
   C.   Mortgage
   D.   Judicial lien

69. What is the bottom piece of a frame that provides a nailing surface for the floor and wall system?

   A.   Eaves
   B.   Joist
   C.   Sill plate
   D.   Stud

70. What is a broker allowed to purchase for a real estate salesperson?

   A.   Phone
   B.   Medical insurance cover
   C.   Retirement plan
   D.   A company vehicle

71. When does a real estate salesperson first provide the agency disclosure form?

   A.   When the deal is about to be closed
   B.   After closing the deal
   C.   First substantial contact
   D.   Never

72. What is the definition of steering?

   A.   When you knowingly provide inaccurate information
   B.   Guiding families with children into an apartment building with other families with children and away from other buildings
   C.   Discriminating against people due to socio-economic status
   D.   Failing to provide proof of continuing real estate education

73. What is the value of a point on a mortgage?

    A.   1% of loan
    B.   5% of the loan
    C.   10% of the loan
    D.   50% of the loan

74. What type of talent are real estate salespeople?

    A.   Assistants
    B.   Independent contractors
    C.   Part time employees
    D.   Full time employees

75. What is the term used to describe a building that is separate from the main house?

    A.   Supplemental structure
    B.   Accessory building
    C.   Secondary land
    D.   Shed

76. The estate that provides absolute ownership of land is called?

    A.   Fee simple estate
    B.   Life estate
    C.   Conditional fee estate
    D.   Legal life estate

77. Which of the following is an example of community property?

    A.   Property that is inherited by the husband through marriage
    B.   Income that is earned by one spouse during the marriage
    C.   Income earned prior to marriage
    D.   A gift given to one spouse during the marriage

78. Fixture are considered _____.

    A.   Hypothecation
    B.   An agreement between the two parties
    C.   Items that are removable by the tenant before the expiration date of the lease
    D.   Real property

79. The commission that is due to a salesperson is decided by?

    A.   Chattels
    B.   State Law
    C.   Mutual Agreement
    D.   Court Decree

80. A real estate broker has become an agent of the seller when ____.

    A.   A listing agreement with the seller has been executed
    B.   They are responsible for sharing commissions
    C.   A broker acts in good faith
    D.   They are procuring cause

81. What is a promissory note?

   A. An agreement between the mortgage company and borrower that shows the terms of the loan

   B. A document that states the buyers intention to buy a property for a specified amount

   C. A note between the broker and buyer stating the exclusive-right-to-represent the buyer

   D. An agreement between the seller and buyer providing a grace period for backing out of the sale

82. _____ occurs when a tenant vacates a premises because the landlord failed to provide essential services.

   A. Quit notices

   B. Actual eviction

   C. Constructive eviction

   D. Notice to quit

83. A buyer has _____ to cancel a contract if a Seller's Disclosure Notice has not been provided prior to the effective date of the contract.?

   A. 9 days

   B. 7 days

   C. 30 days

   D. A Seller's Disclosure Notice is not necessary for buyers

84. Which is not true about the Federal Fair Housing Act?

   A. Prohibits discrimination in housing due to age

   B. Protects people from discrimination when renting or buying a home

   C. Prohibits refusal to sell or rent a house due to familial status

   D. All of the above

85. When a property loses value because of the lack of maintenance on natural wear and tear it is called _____.

    A. External depreciation
    B. Physical deterioration
    C. Economic obsolescence
    D. Negative amortization

THIS IS THE END OF THE NATIONAL PORTION.

STATE PORTION

1. Who has the authority to issue or revoke real estate licenses?

   A. TREC
   B. Texas Governor
   C. TRELA
   D. Broker-Lawyer committee

2. What is the purpose of the Texas Appraiser Licensing & Certification Board (TALCB)?

   A. To safeguard appraisers regarding real estate transactions
   B. To coordinate and create rules for real estate professionals to follow
   C. To manage communications with licensed appraisal professionals
   D. To safeguard consumers regarding matters of real property appraisal services

3. A real estate agent has been issued a penalty for violating TREC rules and regulations. How long does that agent have to pay the penalty?

   A. 7 days
   B. 60 days
   C. 30 days
   D. 1 year

4. Which of the following will cause suspension or revocation of a license?

   A. Guaranteeing future profits
   B. Failing to specify a termination date in a buyer's rep agreement
   C. Giving legal advice to a client
   D. All of the above

5. _____ needs to be displayed in the broker's office and cannot be altered in any way.

    A. Consumer protection notice
    B. Broker's client reviews
    C. Any conflicts of interests
    D. None of the above

6. Where can earnest money be deposited?

    A. Broker's personal account
    B. Broker's operating account
    C. Escrow account
    D. Account set up by the state government

7. Which is not a requirement for obtaining a Texas real estate license?

    A. 18 years of age or older
    B. U.S. citizen or legal alien
    C. Meet TREC's qualifications
    D. A valid driver's license

8. A licensee who has been convicted of a felony must notify the _____.

    A. TRELA
    B. Office of the state governor
    C. TREC
    D. They do not need to notify anyone

9. A broker is responsible for all professional acts of the sponsored salesperson including _____.

   A. Advertising
   B. Use of promulgated forms
   C. Obtaining the sales agent's license
   D. A&B only

10. Texas does not practice _____, which is when a subagent owes the same fiduciary duties as an agent, to the agent's principal?

   A. Dual agency
   B. Subagency
   C. Designated agency
   D. Nonagency

11. What is a substantive dialogue?

   A. A written or in person conversation regarding specific real property
   B. A conversation between seller and buyer regarding any disputes
   C. A dialogue with TREC regarding real estate disputes
   D. A meeting with two real estate agents regarding contract negotiation

12. Which is not considered a fiduciary duty?

   A. Placing the client's interest above their own interest
   B. High duty of care for the client
   C. Duty to the brokerage to bring in client
   D. Honesty and fairness to all parties

13. When a factory causes pollution to a nearby house, the house suffers from _____.

   A. Economic obsolescence
   B. Technological obsolescence
   C. Legal Obsolescence
   D. Aesthetic obsolescence

14. What is the 90-core hour requirement that needs to be met within the first two years of licensing?

   A. State licensing education
   B. Salesman's annual education
   C. Real estate licensee course
   D. No core hour requirement is needed

15. What is a nonresident broker?

   A. A broker who is not a resident of the county they are selling the home in
   B. A broker who has a real estate license in another state, but not in Texas
   C. A broker with a Texas broker's license but with no home or office in Texas
   D. A broker who is not a U.S. citizen

16. What is the term of the disclosure required by the licensed agent who is representing a party?

   A. Property disclosure
   B. Home disclosure
   C. Seller's disclosure
   D. Disclosure of representation

17. Which contract forms are salesperson's and brokers required to use by TREC?

    A. Information about brokerage services
    B. Promulgated contract forms
    C. Seller and buyer contract forms
    D. Seller's disclosure forms

18. Which statute protects consumers against deceptive business practices by sellers, including real estate agents who act fraudulently?

    A. Texas business and commerce code
    B. Homestead exemption
    C. SB 489
    D. Deceptive Trade Practices Act

19. When a person dies without a will, _____ laws govern how property passes.

    A. Intestate succession
    B. Nonagency
    C. Canon of ethics
    D. TRELA

20. Which of the following is a part of the broker licensing requirement?

    A. 2 years of experience
    B. 21 years of age
    C. College degree
    D. 900 classroom education hours

21. TREC requires a licensed broker who is representing a party or is listing real property under an exclusive agreement to do which of the following minimum services?

   A. Inform the party of any material information related to the transaction
   B. Present offers to and from the party
   C. Answer the party's questions
   D. All of the above

22. An unlicensed assistant may do which of the following?

   A. Perform clerical duties
   B. Negotiate earnest money transactions
   C. Show property to clients
   D. Conduct substantive discussions with client

23. Which of the following can cause a license to become inactive?

   A. Failure to conduct real estate transactions for 30 days
   B. Selling person property
   C. Failing to renew the license within the allotted time
   D. Buying property out of state

24. Texas Water Code requires _____ if property is located in a Certificated Service Area of a Utility Service Provider.

   A. A disclosure to the buyer
   B. An additional contract regarding the responsibilities of buying a home in that area
   C. Both A&B
   D. None of the above

25. Texas law allows a minimum of _____ days to cure a default of a foreclosed property before notice of sale can be given.

    A. 20
    B. 30
    C. 60
    D. 90

26. Which form is required when selling property that shares a common boundary with tidally influenced submerged lands of the state?

    A. Addendum for authorizing hydrostatic testing
    B. Addendum for "back-up" contract
    C. Addendum for flood risk property
    D. Addendum for coastal area property

27. What is a short sale addendum?

    A. A contract that involves a home sold at a lower value than the balance of the seller's mortgage loan
    B. The sale of a home where the buyer wants to sell the property quickly
    C. When a home is sold to a buyer who is paying cash
    D. When a buyer needs to take out more than one mortgage to buy a home

28. What is the definition of a broker?

    A. A person who manages the construction of new property
    B. A person who buys property and rents it out to tenants as the landlord
    C. A person who sells, leases or exchanges real estate property
    D. None of the above

29. There are two types of real estate licenses in the state of Texas, the broker license and the salesperson license. Which statement is true about the licenses?

A. A licensee cannot hold both a salesperson license and a broker license
B. The broker license is applicable in all states
C. A licensed salesperson can act as a broker
D. A licensed broker cannot act as a salesperson

30. _____ is when a broker misstates information about material property?

A. Liability
B. Misrepresentation
C. Valuation
D. Mutual recognition

31. Which law states that competing brokers cannot agree to set sale conditions, fees, or management rates?

A. Real Estate Settlement Procedures Act
B. Texas Real Estate License Act
C. Sherman Antitrust Act
D. Timeshare Act

32. In the state of Texas, a _____ is most commonly used to secure a loan when purchasing a home or other real property, similar to mortgages used in other states.

A. Deed of trust
B. Master deed
C. Grantor
D. Closing costs

33. Which statement is not true about becoming a certified residential property manager in Texas?

   A. Must be a registered member of the Texas Association of Realtors
   B. Must take 30 hours of property management education
   C. Must complete the Texas Residential Leasing Specialist (TRLS) certification
   D. All of the above statements are true

34. A mold remediator must give the property owner a certificate of mold remediation within _____ days.

   A. 10
   B. 7
   C. 30
   D. 15

35. _____ is not protected against loss on a standard title insurance policy.

   A. Lack of capacity of the grantor
   B. Forgery in the chain of title
   C. Parties who have possession of superior rights at closing
   D. Encumbrances of record

36. What is a devisee?

   A. A person who is making the will
   B. A person who is transferring the property
   C. The lawyer who is handling the will
   D. The person who is receiving the real property as stated in a will

37. A _____ is when the buyer's contract on a property has been accepted by the seller but the purchase is conditional on the sale of the buyer's current home.

    A.   Active contingent with kick out
    B.   Active contingent without kick out
    C.   Conditional status
    D.   Contingent status

38. A valid lease requires all of the following except:

    A.   Recordation in a county clerk's office
    B.   Valuable consideration
    C.   Capacity to contract
    D.   Offer and acceptance

39. Which is an example of a reasonable modification?

    A.   Changing hardwood floors to carpet
    B.   Lowering kitchen cabinets
    C.   Adding windows
    D.   Repainting the kitchen

40. A(an) _____ allows a landlord to adjust rent under specific economic conditions.

    A.   Escalation clause
    B.   Defeasance clause
    C.   Safety clause
    D.   Contingency clause

THIS IS THE END OF THE STATE PORTION.

Answer Key – National Portion

1.	C	21.	D	41.	B	61.	D	81.	A
2.	A	22.	A	42.	A	62.	B	82.	C
3.	D	23.	C	43.	A	63.	D	83.	B
4.	A	24.	D	44.	C	64.	C	84.	A
5.	C	25.	D	45.	D	65.	A	85.	B
6.	B	26.	A	46.	A	66.	A		
7.	D	27.	A	47.	D	67.	A		
8.	C	28.	A	48.	A	68.	A		
9.	C	29.	B	49.	C	69.	C		
10.	B	30.	A	50.	D	70.	A		
11.	C	31.	B	51.	A	71.	C		
12.	C	32.	A	52.	B	72.	B		
13.	A	33.	B	53.	B	73.	A		
14.	A	34.	B	54.	B	74.	B		
15.	A	35.	A	55.	C	75.	B		
16.	B	36.	B	56.	A	76.	A		
17.	B	37.	B	57.	B	77.	B		
18.	C	38.	C	58.	A	78.	D		
19.	C	39.	C	59.	D	79.	C		
20.	A	40.	B	60.	C	80.	A		

1. **C) Foreclosure**

This is the legal process where a lender seeks to recover the balance of a loan by selling the property held as collateral. Foreclosure usually occurs after a lender has legally obtained a termination of the borrower's right of redemption.

2. **A) Asbestos**

Asbestos is a naturally occurring mineral and its insulation qualities make it popular in making fireproof materials. When products containing asbestos are disturbed, they release tiny fibers in the air that when inhaled over a long period of time can be detrimental as they accumulate in the lung causing scarring and inflammation. Continued exposure affects cells resulting in a rare cancer known as mesothelioma.

3. **D) Studs**

These are vertical beams that are used during construction to frame the house. They are used to form or position walls in a building. Previously, studs made of timber dominated the construction industry but modern construction styles have embraced the use of steel.

4.   **A) Misrepresentation**

Misrepresentation occurs when a broker misstates information of property. It is a false statement that may affect a person's decision to enter into a contract. Three types of misrepresentation are fraudulent misrepresentation, negligent misrepresentation and innocent misrepresentation.

5.   **C) Preventive maintenance**

In order to maintain tenants and an acceptable return on an investment, routine checks and repairs have to be done. These are done to safeguard against failing which may incur losses to the property manager that arise due to cost of replacement.

6.   **B) Mortgagee**

A mortgagee is an entity that lends money for the purpose of buying a real estate property. As a precaution, the mortgagee establishes prior interest in the property and maintains the title as collateral.

7.   **D) $156,250**

$150,000 / (1 - 0.04) = $156,250

8.   **C) Land zoning**

This refers to the restriction of physical development and the use of certain parcels of land. It is done with regard to zoning laws and purposes to protect wildlife and natural resources. It is also used to restrict the number of domestic animals that can be accommodated on a property.

9.   **C) Initiate judicial foreclosure**

Judicial foreclosure are court proceedings that allow the lender to seize the property that was held as collateral for sale. This is done in order to regain the principal amount. This can only be done once it has been established that a defaulting borrower is unable to continue making payments

10.   **B) CERCLA**

This is a trade association that is aimed at trying to improve oversight by representing title insurance. It considers a mortgage a high risk and therefore title insurance must be taken to protect lender

74

11. **C) Fair Credit Reporting Act**

Credit reporting is the process of collecting and analyzing consumers credit information by credit bureaus. This information is sold to lending facilities in order to help them determine whether or not a borrower is eligible for a loan. This act was passed to highlight consumer rights when it comes to credit information.

12. **C) Right of egress**

This is the legal right granted to homeowners as they allow access to property. These rights are usually obtained through an easement and apply regardless of the property type.

13. **A) Sweat equity**

This is the non-monetary equity that owners contribute into the business or property. In this case, sweat equity is the amount of effort an owner puts into a property in order to increase its value.

14. **A) Buydown**

This is a mortgage-financing technique that allows a borrower to negotiate lower monthly payment rates. It usually involves the seller making payments to the lending institution to reduce monthly payment rate of the buyer. As a result, the purchase price goes up.

15. **A) Clear title**

A clear title is a title that has no liens or levies from creditors and other involved parties. A clear title is used to ensure there is no question of ownership. It shows that there are no outstanding financial responsibilities attached to the property and the owner is legally capable of selling the property.

16. **B) Credit report**

A credit report is a detailed breakdown of an individual's credit history and is usually carried out by credit bureaus. They use financial information attached to an individual like their bill payment to establish a unique report. This information is usually used by lenders while considering a loan applicant.

17. **B) Equity**

Equity is another term for ownership. In home investments, equity means the amount of principal that has been paid off. The higher the equity the easier it is to refinance a property.

18.   **C) Notice of default**

This is a public notice filed in court regarding a borrower's default on a loan. It is usually to notify the borrower that there has been a breach in the contractual limit that had been predetermined in the loan. A grace period is included for negotiation before further action is considered.

19.   **C) Lock-in period**

This is the period usually 30 to 60 days within which a lender is required to keep a loan offer open. This gives the borrower enough time to prepare for closing while the lender is processing the loan. A lock in period protects the borrower from losses incurred throughout the repayment of the loan caused by rising interest rates during processing of the loan.

20.   **A) When a tenant breaks a rent prior to the date of expiry without a legal reason.**

As a lease is a contract, breaking a lease without a valid reason may result in being sued by the landlord. To avoid legal action, the individual breaking the lease must prove beyond reasonable doubt that the break was caused by a situation completely out of their hands.

21.   **D) Shortfall**

Shortfall is a term used to describe a situation where a financial obligation exceeds the required amount of cash available. A shortfall may be a temporary and current situation or a prolonged one. The latter represents mismanagement of funds and warrants a deeper look into spending habits and change has to be implemented.

22.   **A) Tax abatement**

Tax abatement is a strategy used by the government to increase investments in specific areas. In the real estate sector, tax abatement occurs when taxes on properties are significantly reduced or completely eliminated. It is usually done to encourage investors to buy property in areas that have recorded long term low demand.

23.   **C) $546,000**

$500,000 * 1.04 * 1.05 = $546,000

24.   **D) Department of Health**

25.   **D) $368,000**

$92,000 / 0.25 = $368,000

76

26. **A) Abstract of title**

This is a summarized history of all title transfers and legal actions that have been connected with a certain property. It is beneficial in preventing home buyers from getting tangled in legal issues that are attached to a property. This is because any loss made because of a court ruling on a property once a buyer has purchased will be incurred by the new tenant.

27. **A) Flashing**

This is a material used to cover joints where two or more types of material join. This usually happens to prevent water leakage through the joint. It also provides a drainage between two joints.

28. **A) Eaves**

This is a part of the roof that projects over the wall beyond the edge of the roof. It is usually set in place to channel water away from the roof.

29. **B) Cash on cash return**

Cash on cash return that a proven metric used to calculate future cash returns on a cash investment. This metric is only true for a cash investment and does not take into account loan investments.

30. **A) Architectural Review Board**

The Architectural Review Board is given the responsibility of upholding the visual integrity of a town. It is responsible for reviewing all exterior designs of all residential and commercial structures in a town. All new structures and structures that are up for alteration are required to provide a blueprint of the exterior design for printing. They are also charged with ensuring commercial signs conform to the towns design.

31. **B) Gross lease**

A gross lease is a lease where a flat rent fee is paid. It includes rent and other utility fees such as taxes and insurance. A landlord is obligated to calculate a rate based on history or research. A negotiation between the tenant and landlord can also be reached on the services the tenant wants to be included in the lease.

32. **A) House rules**

These are rules that are given to tenants of a coop or condo on the beginning of the contract regarding behavior within the complex. They are put in place to ensure a comfortable living space for all occupants. Failure to adhere to the rules may result in eviction.

33. **B) Absorption rate**

This is a ration of the number of properties that have been sold against the number of properties that are available for sale within a specified area.

34. **B) Acceleration clause**

This is a provision in a mortgage that allows the lender the right to demand the immediate settlement on a mortgage under certain predetermined conditions such as a borrower defaulting on a loan.

35. **A) Easement appurtenant**

Easement appurtenant is an agreement that is transferable with ownership rights of a property. When a property is transferred through sale or inheritance, all rights and privileges attached to the land are automatically transferred to the new owner.

36. **B) Homeowner's warranty insurance**

Homeowner's warranty insurance insures the homeowner from the builder's faults for a specified warranty period

37. **B) Adverse possession**

This is a legal principle that allows a person who has been living on a specific land for a long period of time to take possession of the land without permission of the owner. The individual does not have to have a title to the land to acquire it. The title holder is capable of claiming his land by choosing to eject the squatter.

38. **C) Encumbrance**

This is a limitation against a real estate property. It restricts the owner from transferring ownership of the title. It also prevents an owner from depreciating the value of the property.

39. **C) Joists**

These are horizontal structural members used to frame an open space. They are often used in transferring loads to the vertical members of the structure. When used in floors, they provide stiffness in the framing systems.

40. **B) Conveyance**

A conveyance or sale deed is a legally binding contract that transfers all ownership rights from the seller to the buyer. It usually states the agreed-on price, the date of the transaction and the obligations of the parties involved.

41. **B) Non-solicitation order**

This is an order issued to broker and agents to prevent them from soliciting listings in designated areas

42. **A) Colleges**

Despite the fact that all property is assessed to determine its value, universities, schools, parks, government institutions, religious organizations, and hospitals are exempt from property taxes. Veterans are also eligible from partial exemption from taxes.

43. **A) Accountability**

Commingling is a contract breach where a fiduciary mixed funds belonging to a client with his own making it impossible to separate them. The accountability clause requires a fiduciary to be able to maintain an accurate report of documents and funds that he/she has been entrusted.

44. **C) Eminent domain**

This is the government's power to take private land for public use under certain circumstances. It is defined by the Taking Clause of the Fifth Amendment which prohibits the taking of private land without just compensation. It emphasizes that the government can only take land for public use and offer just compensation on the land.

45. **D) Refuse modifications for handicapped tenants**

Refuse to allow tenants to make reasonable structural modifications to a unit at the tenant's expense to allow the handicapped tenant full enjoyment of the property (Fair Housing Act). In accordance with the Fair Housing Act which is against discrimination in housing, multifamily buildings are expected to ensure accessibility for people using wheelchairs

46. **A) The Americans with Disabilities Act of 1990**

This act was enacted to ensure disabled people are not discriminated against and have equal rights regarding access to employment and commercial facilities.

47. **D) Tenancy at will**

This is a tenancy that is not bound by a lease and does not have an expiry or duration of tenancy. A predetermined payment plan is adhered and a tenant is flexible to terminate the tenancy without legal proceedings. It is a beneficial plan for landlords and tenants that seek flexibility.

48. **A) $2,041**

($350,000 * 0.07) / 12 = $2,041

49. **C) Civil Rights Act Amendment of 1974**

The Civil Rights act amendment of 1974 banned discrimination based on sex and credit in a congress proceeding. Women being offered maternity leave on the assumption that they were unable to work was rendered illegal and sexist teaching methods were discredited.

50. **D) Handicaps and familial status**

The act protects people with disabilities and families with children. Pregnant women were also protected from illegal discrimination.

51. **A) $70,000**

$500,000 * 0.14 = $70,000

52. **B) Assessor**

An assessor is a government official that is engaged to determine the value of a property. The information gathered by an assessor is used to calculate future property taxes. Assessors maintain annual assessments at a uniform percentage of market value.

53. **B) Amortization**

This is the scheduling of monthly mortgage payments showing breakdown of payment. When paying a mortgage loan for a property, the initial payments are put towards paying off the interest and less is allocated to the principal amount. As a borrower makes more payments, more is allocated to the principal and less to the interest.

54. **B) Real estate tax**

This is an ad valorem tax on the value of a property. It is levied annually on real estate by the government authority.

55. **C) Leverage**

This refers to money that has been borrowed to finance an investment property. The leverage concept works best when rent and property values are on the rise. Monthly mortgage payments for the rental property become constant which results in a rise in profits

56. **A) Forced air system**

A forced air system refers to any HVAC system that makes use of air ducts and vents to release temperature-controlled air into the building. A forced air system released filtered and dehumidified cold air into buildings and runs at an affordable price. A central air system on the other hand uses vents in the forced air system to provide cool and conditioned air.

57. **B) One year**

An individual is required to wait for an entire year after which the agent is required to prove with evidence that he/she is capable of being trustworthy and upholding the law with regard to the real estate sector.

58. **A) Board of directors**

A co-op is an alternative method to traditional housing. A board of directors is elected by the shareholders to run the corporation. They are responsible for vetting and doing background checks on potential new shareholders in the corporation. They are also responsible for upholding the values and regulations of the co-op and terminating tenancy of individuals found to be acting contrary to the rules.

59. **D) Abstraction method**

This is a method of estimating the value of a piece of land that is based on the going price of similar parcels of land within the area.

60. **C) Grantor**

This is the party that transfers ownership of property to buyer through a legal document known as a deed. The grantor is required to sign the deed admitting the transfer of ownership before closing. The deed is then filed at the county jurisdiction for public record.

61. **D) Radon**

Radon is a radioactive cancer-causing gas that comes from the natural breakdown of uranium in soil. The gas penetrates its way into houses from cracks and holes in the foundation. Testing for radon gas is mandatory during purchasing of a home in order to fix the problem by lowering the amount of radon gas available to the acceptable amounts.

62. **B) Riparian rights**

These are rights that arise when an individual owns land near a moving watercourse. These rights include swimming and irrigation. The rights only attach when there's a water on one side of the land. An individual is allowed to benefit from the water body without contaminating or altering the flow of the waterbody.

63. **D) Regulation Z**

It requires lenders to make comprehensive disclosure statements to borrowers for consumer loans. It is aimed at protecting consumers from misleading lending practices. Lenders are required to disclose interest rates, finance charges, explain terms used and respond to all complaints launched by the borrower. This law was passed to ensure that borrowers make informed credit choices.

64. **C) Right of first refusal**

This is the right given to a specific party to purchase or lease a property before it is open to bidding by other potential buyers. The party being offered the privilege is not obligated to buy the property. In the event that the party is not interested in the property, it is opened up to the public.

65. **A) Economic obsolescence**

This is the decrease in the market value of a property due to external factors that cannot be controlled by the property owner i.e. building of an interstate highway close to a prime property. Its value immediately decreases due to the noise pollution.

66. **A) Special agent**

A special agent is an agent whose services are only employed for a specific task. Once the task is completed a special agent no longer has authority to represent the client.

67. **A) Appraisal**

An appraisal in a professional opinion value assessment of a property and is independent of the market values of similar properties based on the fact that all properties are unique and cannot be compared to each other.

68. **A) Mechanic's lien**

This is a security interest in title of property for the benefit of those who supplied materials and offered professional services on the construction and renovation of a property. A mechanic's lien can be taken on both real and personal properties.

69. **C) Sill plate**

This is a horizontal member of a wall where vertical members of the building are attached. It usually lies between the foundation and floor frame.

70. **A) Phone**

This is because salespeople are considered independent contractors and therefore are not eligible for company benefits.

71. **C) First substantial contact**

This refers to the earliest practicable opportunity during a conversation with the consumer. An agency disclosure is to be provided to disclose and explain the nature of the representation in a real estate transaction.

72. **B) Guiding families with children into an apartment building with other families with children and away from other buildings**

Steering is an unlawful practice that violates the federal fair housing provisions. It is a practice in which brokers influence the choice of a prospective buyer or tenant.

73. **A) 1% of loan**

A value point is a fee paid directly to the lender at closing in exchange for a reduced interest rate and can lower a borrower's monthly mortgage payment.

74. **B) Independent contractors**

Independent contractors are hired to perform a service but are not included in the employee catalogue. Their main goal is to complete the task and the employing broker has no control over the process of yielding results or financial expenses incurred.

75. **B) Accessory building**

This is a building that is built separately from the main structure in a property. It is usually put to use for a specific purpose such as a shed, workshop or garage.

76. **A) Fee simple estate**

This provides absolute ownership of the land and allows the owner to do whatever they choose to with the land. This is the highest form of ownership in real estate.

77. **B) Income that is earned by one spouse during the marriage**

Community property is defined as everything that a married couple owns together. This includes income and property acquired during the duration of the marriage.

78. **D) Real property**

A fixture is physically property that is permanently attached to real property (on it or under it), that cannot be moved. Examples include ponds, canals, buildings and roads.

79. **C) Mutual Agreement**

An agreement between a buyer and a seller. It is a binding contract between the two parties and includes any contingencies.

80. **A) A listing agreement with the seller has been executed**

A listing agreement is a contract between the homeowner and a selling agent. It is a legal agreement that gives the selling agent the right to sell the home.

81. **A) An agreement between the mortgage company and borrower that shows the terms of the loan**

This binding note states the terms of the loan and that the borrower promises to for the loan. It also provides evidence of the loan and both parties must sign the note to make it legally binding.

82. **C) Constructive eviction**

A constructive eviction is when a tenant must move out because the landlord fails to do something which renders the property uninhabitable. The tenant needs to give notice of the condition and allow a reasonable amount of time for the landlord to fix it. If this does not occur, the tenant can move out.

83. **B) 7 days**

If a seller's disclosure notice is not provided to the buyer, then they buyer has 7 days to cancel the contract.

84. **A) Prohibits discrimination in housing due to age**

The Federal Fair Housing Law prohibits discrimination due to race, color, national origin, religion, sex, familiar status and disability. This act prohibits discrimination when renting or buying a home, getting a mortgage, seeking housing assistance or engaging in other housing-related activities.

85. **B) Physical deterioration**

This is the most obvious form of depreciation and can occur when maintenance does not keep up with natural wear and tear. It causes a loss of value to the property. There are two types of physical deterioration functional obsolescence and external obsolescence.

Answer Key – State Portion

1.	A	21.	D
2.	D	22.	A
3.	C	23.	C
4.	D	24.	A
5.	A	25.	A
6.	C	26.	D
7.	D	27.	A
8.	C	28.	C
9.	D	29.	A
10.	B	30.	B
11.	A	31.	C
12.	C	32.	A
13.	A	33.	B
14.	B	34.	A
15.	C	35.	C
16.	D	36.	D
17.	B	37.	D
18.	D	38.	A
19.	A	39.	B
20.	D	40.	A

1. **A) TREC**

   TREC regulates licensed brokerages, inspectors, residential service companies and entities that offer timeshare interests. Prior to TREC licenses were issued and revoked by the securities division of the Secretary of State's office.

2. **D) To safeguard consumers regarding matters of real property appraisal services**

   TALB works with TREC to oversees real estate brokerage, real property appraisals, inspections, home warranties and timeshare opportunities. TALB also provides licensing services, education, and enforces laws the govern real proper appraisals.

3. **C) 30 days**

   The violator has 30 days to pay the penalty. TREC can administer penalties for each day the violation continues.

4.   **D) All of the above**

These are all reasons a licensee can have their license revoked or suspended. These examples fail to comply with TREC rules and regulations.

5.   **A) Consumer protection notice**

This form notifies the public of the recovery trust account and needs to be noticeable on a brokers homepage, including any social media pages, i.e. Facebook. It also needs to be posted at the brokerage office and cannot be altered in any way, including font style and size.

6.   **C) Escrow account**

Earnest money must be deposited into an escrow account and is credited towards the buyer's down payment. If the transaction is terminated, then the earnest money can go to the seller.

7.   **D) A valid driver's license**

A real estate agent does not need to have a valid driver's license, but they need to find a broker sponsorship to be able to perform real estate services.

8.   **C) TREC**

The licensee must notify Texas Real Estate Commission and they must notify them within 30 days of the conviction.

9.   **D) A&B only**

A broker who sponsors the sales agent is responsible for all professional acts of the agent. This includes any advertising, use of real estate forms and any proper disclosures needed.

10.   **B) Subagency**

Not practiced in Texas, subagency occurs when a sales associate from another brokerage shows property to a buyer. The subagent works with the buyer and owes the fiduciary duties to the listing broker and seller.

11.   **A) A written or in person conversation regarding specific real property**

This dialogue does not include conversations at open houses. An example of a substantive dialogue is a conversation with a prospective client regarding properties. Written (email or other electronic messaging) conversations regarding a specified property is considered substantive dialogue as well.

12.   **C) Duty to the brokerage to bring in clients**

The fiduciary relationship includes attorneys, trustees, investment brokers and real estate agents. The duty is owed to the principal of the license holder.

13.   **A) Economic obsolescence**

Economic obsolescence is depreciation cause by outside factors or factors on, in or within the property lines. Job market and crime are examples of economic obsolescence.

14.   **B) Salesman's annual education**

The required education that a licensee needs to complete during their first two years of being a licensed agent in order to renew the license.

15.   **C) A broker with a Texas broker's license but with no home or office in Texas**

A nonresident broker is licensed through TREC. Although they are licensed, they need to work for a brokerage that is a resident broker in Texas.

16.   **D) Disclosure of representation**

Disclosure must be oral or written and must disclose that they represent the buyer when making an appointment with a listing agent or seller to show property.

17.   **B) Promulgated contract forms**

These forms are written by the broker-lawyer committee and disbursed by TREC to agents and brokers. These forms must be used to make transaction agreements official.

18.   **D) Deceptive Trade Practices Act**

This act is the primary consumer protection statute. It prohibits deceptive trade practices which are false or misleading and gives the consumers the right to sue for damages. Consumers have 2 years from when they discover the deception to file a complaint.

19.   **A) Intestate succession**

This determines how property is distributed upon death without a will. This occurs even when a will makes a partial distribution of the property.

20.   **D) 900 classroom hours**

Agents who wish to be brokers must have 4 years of experience in Texas as a licensed sales agent. They must also have 3600 points of qualifying practical experience as required by the rules of the Texas real estate commission.

21.   **D) All of the above**

TREC requires licensed agents and brokers to follow a canon of ethics as well as provide minimum services. Refraining from telling another broker to negotiate directly with the broker's client is also a minimum service required by licensed brokers.

22.   **A) Perform clerical duties**

Along with performing clerical duties, an unlicensed assistant can act as a greeter at an open house. They also must be careful and not perform activities that require a license.

23.   **C) Failing to renew the license within the allotted time**

If a licensee fails to renew their license TREC will move the license to an inactive state. TREC can also administer monetary fines for failing to renew a license i.e. a licensee renews their license on time but does not include the required education. This will cause the licensee to be fined.

24.   **A) A disclosure to buyers**

A disclosure needs to be made to buyers stating that there may be a charge for water and sewer services.

25.   **A) 20**

A notice of default and intent to accelerate must be sent to the borrower which notifies the borrower of the minimum of 20-day notice. Quasi-judicial law is required for foreclosures on home equity loans.

26.   **D) Addendum for coastal area property**

This form is required when selling property in coastal areas by the Texas Natural Resource Code in all types of transactions. This form can be found on the TREC website.

27.   **A) A contract that involves a home sold at a lower value than the balance of the seller's mortgage loan**

A short sale is when a home is sold at a lower value than the balance of the seller's mortgage. This type of sale requires consent from the lienholder. Texas requires an addendum form be filled out in short sales, which provides details regarding the sale.

28.   **C) A person who sells, leases or exchanges real estate property**

A broker lists real estate with the intent of selling, leasing or exchanging it. They also control the deposit of rent and are required to follow TREC guidelines.

29. **A) A licensee cannot hold both a salesperson license and a broker license**

The license act does not allow a licensee to hold both a salesperson license and a broker license at the same time. It does allow a licensed broker to act as both a broker and a salesperson.

30. **B) Misrepresentation**

A broker can be sued for misrepresentation. This includes failure to disclose or reveal material feature of property or a false statement regarding the property.

31. **C) Sherman Antitrust Act**

This law prohibits tie-in agreements, price fixing, group boycotting and the allocation of customers or markets.

32. **A) Deed of trust**

The deed of trust is used to transfer interest in real property. It can also be used as a permanent part of a comprehensive estate plan, but the trustee must meet the legal requirements listed by the state of Texas.

33. **B) Must take 30 hours of property management education**

The property manager must take only 4 three-hour courses. The property manager must also complete an application which will include a verification of over 200-unit years of residential management experience over at least a 2-year period.

34. **A) 10**

The certificate must be given to the property owner within 10 days. It must include a statement saying that the contamination has been remediated by the assessor.

35. **C) Parties who have possession of superior rights at closing**

The title insurance company does not do a physical check of the property. They only check the public records, because of this, the insurance company does not insure against parties in possession.

36. **D) The person who is receiving the real property as stated in a will**

A devisee is the one who is receiving the real property while the testator is the one who makes the will and transfers the real property.

37.   **D) Contingent status**

The contingent status is when the buyer's purchase is contingent upon the sale of the buyer's home. The two types of contingent statues are active contingent with kick out which means the seller can kick out the current contract if a better offer comes around and the active contingent without kick out which means the seller cannot force the hand of the current buyer or accept another offer.

38.   **A) Recordation in a county clerk's office**

It is not necessary to have a lease be recorded at the county court office to deem it valid, but many commercial leases are recorded to give constructive notice of the lease.

39.   **B) Lowering kitchen cabinets**

Lowering kitchen cabinets, making structural modifications so disabled people could enjoy the units and installing grab bars are examples of reasonable modifications. A landlord is required to allow a tenant to make these modifications at the tenant's expense but must return the property to its original state if they affect a person's use.

40.   **A) Escalation clause**

This clause allows a landlord to adjust the rent of a tent. This is typically tied into an increase in service or cost of living index.

Practice Test 3

Directions:

1. You have a 150-minute time limit for the national portion, and a 90-minute time limit for the state portion.

2. To pass, you must answer at least 56 out of 85 questions correctly on the national portion **AND** at least 21 out of 40 questions on the state portion.

3. Some questions will require mathematics. You may use a calculator.

4. **Phones and pagers are not allowed. Having either will result in automatic dismissal from the exam and nullification of exam scores.**

Tips:

- Answer all questions even if you are unsure.
- Mark any questions you are stuck on and revisit them after you are done. The exam is timed so make sure you finish as many questions as you can.
- After reading the question, try answering it in your head first to avoid getting confused by the choices.
- Read the entire question before looking at the answers.
- Use the process of elimination to filter out choices that don't seem correct to increase your chances of selecting the correct answer.
- Be aware of important keywords like **not, sometimes, always,** and **never**. These words completely alter the ask of the question so it's important to keep track of them.

PLEASE READ THESE INSTRUCTIONS CAREFULLY.

Name: _____   Date: _____

NATIONAL PORTION

1.	Ⓐ Ⓑ Ⓒ Ⓓ	31. Ⓐ Ⓑ Ⓒ Ⓓ	61. Ⓐ Ⓑ Ⓒ Ⓓ
2.	Ⓐ Ⓑ Ⓒ Ⓓ	32. Ⓐ Ⓑ Ⓒ Ⓓ	62. Ⓐ Ⓑ Ⓒ Ⓓ
3.	Ⓐ Ⓑ Ⓒ Ⓓ	33. Ⓐ Ⓑ Ⓒ Ⓓ	63. Ⓐ Ⓑ Ⓒ Ⓓ
4.	Ⓐ Ⓑ Ⓒ Ⓓ	34. Ⓐ Ⓑ Ⓒ Ⓓ	64. Ⓐ Ⓑ Ⓒ Ⓓ
5.	Ⓐ Ⓑ Ⓒ Ⓓ	35. Ⓐ Ⓑ Ⓒ Ⓓ	65. Ⓐ Ⓑ Ⓒ Ⓓ
6.	Ⓐ Ⓑ Ⓒ Ⓓ	36. Ⓐ Ⓑ Ⓒ Ⓓ	66. Ⓐ Ⓑ Ⓒ Ⓓ
7.	Ⓐ Ⓑ Ⓒ Ⓓ	37. Ⓐ Ⓑ Ⓒ Ⓓ	67. Ⓐ Ⓑ Ⓒ Ⓓ
8.	Ⓐ Ⓑ Ⓒ Ⓓ	38. Ⓐ Ⓑ Ⓒ Ⓓ	68. Ⓐ Ⓑ Ⓒ Ⓓ
9.	Ⓐ Ⓑ Ⓒ Ⓓ	39. Ⓐ Ⓑ Ⓒ Ⓓ	69. Ⓐ Ⓑ Ⓒ Ⓓ
10.	Ⓐ Ⓑ Ⓒ Ⓓ	40. Ⓐ Ⓑ Ⓒ Ⓓ	70. Ⓐ Ⓑ Ⓒ Ⓓ
11.	Ⓐ Ⓑ Ⓒ Ⓓ	41. Ⓐ Ⓑ Ⓒ Ⓓ	71. Ⓐ Ⓑ Ⓒ Ⓓ
12.	Ⓐ Ⓑ Ⓒ Ⓓ	42. Ⓐ Ⓑ Ⓒ Ⓓ	72. Ⓐ Ⓑ Ⓒ Ⓓ
13.	Ⓐ Ⓑ Ⓒ Ⓓ	43. Ⓐ Ⓑ Ⓒ Ⓓ	73. Ⓐ Ⓑ Ⓒ Ⓓ
14.	Ⓐ Ⓑ Ⓒ Ⓓ	44. Ⓐ Ⓑ Ⓒ Ⓓ	74. Ⓐ Ⓑ Ⓒ Ⓓ
15.	Ⓐ Ⓑ Ⓒ Ⓓ	45. Ⓐ Ⓑ Ⓒ Ⓓ	75. Ⓐ Ⓑ Ⓒ Ⓓ
16.	Ⓐ Ⓑ Ⓒ Ⓓ	46. Ⓐ Ⓑ Ⓒ Ⓓ	76. Ⓐ Ⓑ Ⓒ Ⓓ
17	Ⓐ Ⓑ Ⓒ Ⓓ	47. Ⓐ Ⓑ Ⓒ Ⓓ	77. Ⓐ Ⓑ Ⓒ Ⓓ
18.	Ⓐ Ⓑ Ⓒ Ⓓ	48. Ⓐ Ⓑ Ⓒ Ⓓ	78. Ⓐ Ⓑ Ⓒ Ⓓ
19.	Ⓐ Ⓑ Ⓒ Ⓓ	49. Ⓐ Ⓑ Ⓒ Ⓓ	79. Ⓐ Ⓑ Ⓒ Ⓓ
20.	Ⓐ Ⓑ Ⓒ Ⓓ	50. Ⓐ Ⓑ Ⓒ Ⓓ	80. Ⓐ Ⓑ Ⓒ Ⓓ
21.	Ⓐ Ⓑ Ⓒ Ⓓ	51. Ⓐ Ⓑ Ⓒ Ⓓ	81. Ⓐ Ⓑ Ⓒ Ⓓ
22.	Ⓐ Ⓑ Ⓒ Ⓓ	52. Ⓐ Ⓑ Ⓒ Ⓓ	82. Ⓐ Ⓑ Ⓒ Ⓓ
23.	Ⓐ Ⓑ Ⓒ Ⓓ	53. Ⓐ Ⓑ Ⓒ Ⓓ	83. Ⓐ Ⓑ Ⓒ Ⓓ
24.	Ⓐ Ⓑ Ⓒ Ⓓ	54. Ⓐ Ⓑ Ⓒ Ⓓ	84. Ⓐ Ⓑ Ⓒ Ⓓ
25.	Ⓐ Ⓑ Ⓒ Ⓓ	55. Ⓐ Ⓑ Ⓒ Ⓓ	85. Ⓐ Ⓑ Ⓒ Ⓓ
26.	Ⓐ Ⓑ Ⓒ Ⓓ	56. Ⓐ Ⓑ Ⓒ Ⓓ	
27.	Ⓐ Ⓑ Ⓒ Ⓓ	57. Ⓐ Ⓑ Ⓒ Ⓓ	
28.	Ⓐ Ⓑ Ⓒ Ⓓ	58. Ⓐ Ⓑ Ⓒ Ⓓ	
29.	Ⓐ Ⓑ Ⓒ Ⓓ	59. Ⓐ Ⓑ Ⓒ Ⓓ	
30.	Ⓐ Ⓑ Ⓒ Ⓓ	60. Ⓐ Ⓑ Ⓒ Ⓓ	

Name: _____   Date: _____

STATE PORTION

1.	Ⓐ	Ⓑ	Ⓒ	Ⓓ
2.	Ⓐ	Ⓑ	Ⓒ	Ⓓ
3.	Ⓐ	Ⓑ	Ⓒ	Ⓓ
4.	Ⓐ	Ⓑ	Ⓒ	Ⓓ
5.	Ⓐ	Ⓑ	Ⓒ	Ⓓ
6.	Ⓐ	Ⓑ	Ⓒ	Ⓓ
7.	Ⓐ	Ⓑ	Ⓒ	Ⓓ
8.	Ⓐ	Ⓑ	Ⓒ	Ⓓ
9.	Ⓐ	Ⓑ	Ⓒ	Ⓓ
10.	Ⓐ	Ⓑ	Ⓒ	Ⓓ
11.	Ⓐ	Ⓑ	Ⓒ	Ⓓ
12.	Ⓐ	Ⓑ	Ⓒ	Ⓓ
13.	Ⓐ	Ⓑ	Ⓒ	Ⓓ
14.	Ⓐ	Ⓑ	Ⓒ	Ⓓ
15.	Ⓐ	Ⓑ	Ⓒ	Ⓓ
16.	Ⓐ	Ⓑ	Ⓒ	Ⓓ
17	Ⓐ	Ⓑ	Ⓒ	Ⓓ
18.	Ⓐ	Ⓑ	Ⓒ	Ⓓ
19.	Ⓐ	Ⓑ	Ⓒ	Ⓓ
20.	Ⓐ	Ⓑ	Ⓒ	Ⓓ
21.	Ⓐ	Ⓑ	Ⓒ	Ⓓ
22.	Ⓐ	Ⓑ	Ⓒ	Ⓓ
23.	Ⓐ	Ⓑ	Ⓒ	Ⓓ
24.	Ⓐ	Ⓑ	Ⓒ	Ⓓ
25.	Ⓐ	Ⓑ	Ⓒ	Ⓓ
26.	Ⓐ	Ⓑ	Ⓒ	Ⓓ
27.	Ⓐ	Ⓑ	Ⓒ	Ⓓ
28.	Ⓐ	Ⓑ	Ⓒ	Ⓓ
29.	Ⓐ	Ⓑ	Ⓒ	Ⓓ
30.	Ⓐ	Ⓑ	Ⓒ	Ⓓ

31.	Ⓐ	Ⓑ	Ⓒ	Ⓓ
32.	Ⓐ	Ⓑ	Ⓒ	Ⓓ
33.	Ⓐ	Ⓑ	Ⓒ	Ⓓ
34.	Ⓐ	Ⓑ	Ⓒ	Ⓓ
35.	Ⓐ	Ⓑ	Ⓒ	Ⓓ
36.	Ⓐ	Ⓑ	Ⓒ	Ⓓ
37.	Ⓐ	Ⓑ	Ⓒ	Ⓓ
38.	Ⓐ	Ⓑ	Ⓒ	Ⓓ
39.	Ⓐ	Ⓑ	Ⓒ	Ⓓ
40.	Ⓐ	Ⓑ	Ⓒ	Ⓓ

NATIONAL PORTION

1. What is the name given to the estimate amount on a mortgage?

   A. Pre-approval
   B. Post-approval
   C. Principal
   D. Mortgage

2. What is the actual amount of space a tenant can lay carpet and place furniture?

   A. Usable Square Footage
   B. Rentable square footage
   C. Common areas
   D. Service areas

3. What is the name given to an amount of money borrowed to facilitate the purchase of a property?

   A. Escrow
   B. Interest
   C. Down payment
   D. Principal

4. What type of mortgage loan is made available through the United States Department of Veterans Affairs?

   A. Blanket mortgage
   B. Balloon mortgage
   C. Graduated mortgage
   D. VA mortgage

5. What is the value obtained by deducting applied payments from original amortization?

   A. Full term
   B. Paid term
   C. Principal term
   D. Remaining term

6. What is the arrangement that allows a seller to lease a property from a purchaser after selling it?

   A. Leaseback
   B. Leasehold
   C. Sublease
   D. Proprietary lease

7. What type of easement attaches rights to a tenant instead of the land?

   A. Easement appurtenant
   B. Easement in gross
   C. Prescriptive easement
   D. All the above

8. What is the penalty charge for paying back a loan ahead of the scheduled payment plan?

   A. Defaulting penalty
   B. Interest
   C. Prepayment penalty
   D. Principal amount

9. What is an insurance premium paid by the buyer to the lender in order to protect the lender from default on a mortgage?

   A. Hazard insurance
   B. Homeowner's insurance
   C. Private mortgage insurance
   D. Title insurance

10. What is the name given to a party that acts in conjunction with a lender to originate a loan?

   A. Mortgage broker
   B. Third party originator
   C. Lender
   D. Intermediate

11. What is the term used to describe the alteration of a property in order to increase its market value?

   A. Capital Improvement
   B. Preventive maintenance
   C. Appreciation
   D. Common charges

12. What is the tax levied on transfer of property?

   A. Capital gains tax
   B. Deductible tax
   C. Property tax
   D. Transfer tax

13. Which of the following is an appraisal method in real estate?

   A. Sales Comparison Approach
   B. Cost Approach
   C. Income Approach
   D. All of the above

14. For at least how long must an asset be held before being sold to be categorized as long-term capital gains?

   A. One month
   B. Six months
   C. One year
   D. Two years

15. Which of these is considered an operating expense?

   A. Repairs
   B. Depreciation
   C. Payroll
   D. All of the above

16. What is an unlawful detainer?

   A. Forcing rent payments for tenants who have already moved out
   B. Refusing to leave a property despite expiration or termination of lease
   C. Listing a property whose lease has not expired
   D. Subletting a property without permission from the landlord

17. What is the freeze placed on a mortgage loan for a period of time?

  A. Cessation
  B. Amortization
  C. Rate lock
  D. Interest freeze

18. What type of lease gives the tenant an option to purchase the property?

  A. Leaseback
  B. Lease option
  C. Leasehold
  D. Gross lease

19. What is conditioner capacity?

  A. This is the capacity of an air conditioner to heat or cool the room
  B. The space used up by an air conditioner
  C. The strength of an air conditioner
  D. The cooling capacity of an air conditioner and is measured in tons

20. What is the name given to an individual that acts in intermediate for brokers and lenders?

  A. Mortgage broker
  B. Mortgage banker
  C. Attorney
  D. Intermediate

21. If a property is taxed at 30% with a tax levy of $105,000, what is its assessed value?

  A. $136,500
  B. $146,666
  C. $350,000
  D. None of the above

22. What is the notice given when a tenant has a pet in a complex that has no pets policy?

  A. Notice to cure
  B. Notice to quit
  C. Notice of default
  D. Notice of termination

23. What is a roof's vertical rise in inches divided by its horizontal span in feet?

  A. Depth
  B. Width
  C. Pitch
  D. Length

24. Who engages the services of a broker?

  A. The client
  B. The neighbor
  C. The contractor
  D. The appraiser

25. Right of way would be best defined as?

    A. Escheat
    B. Easement
    C. Right of ingress
    D. Encumbrance

26. Who can get partial exemptions from property taxes?

    A. Disabled
    B. Schools
    C. Shelters
    D. Markets

27. What age must a person be to get a Real Estate license?

    A. 16 years
    B. 18 years
    C. 30 years
    D. 43 years

28. Which electricity conductor plays the same role as a circuit board?

    A. Cell
    B. Capacitor
    C. Fuse
    D. Switch

29. What is the definition of a bilateral contract?

    A. A contract that involves only the promisor
    B. A contract that involves only the promisee
    C. A contract that involves both a promisor and promisee
    D. A contract that allows both parties to drop all claims and get out of the contract

30. What is real property tax based on?

    A. Assessed value
    B. CMA
    C. Appraisal
    D. Taxable value

31. What agency is responsible for protecting wetlands?

    A. CERCLA
    B. Environmental Protection Agency
    C. FEMA
    D. NY Health Department

32. What is a schedule of the projected future income and expenses for a real estate investment?

    A. IOU
    B. Invoice
    C. Promissory note
    D. Pro Forma Statement

33. What is an agent required to do if a client refuses to sign an agency disclosure form?

   A. Terminate relationship
   B. Create record of refusal in writing
   C. Continue without record of the refusal
   D. Take legal action against the client

34. What is a general voluntary lien?

   A. Mortgage
   B. Taxes
   C. Revenues
   D. Duties

35. If a salesperson's commission is not paid, he resorts to?

   A. Buyer
   B. Seller
   C. Broker
   D. Lender

36. What type of tenancy exists where property is owned by a single individual?

   A. Joint tenancy
   B. Ownership in severalty
   C. Tenancy in entirety
   D. Tenancy in common

37. Who are testers in real estate?

   A. People who pose as real estate clients to check if fair housing is being practiced
   B. People who assess the value of a property
   C. People who pose as borrowers to ensure proper loaning practices
   D. People who approach the seller without the intention of buying

38. What is the term used to describe the natural increase of land?

   A. Expansion
   B. Avulsion
   C. Erosion
   D. Accretion

39. What is the length of time allowed for depreciation for a residential property?

   A. 5 years
   B. 27.5 years
   C. 39 years
   D. 70 years

40. What is the term used to describe personal property?

   A. Chattel
   B. Investment
   C. Possession
   D. Real property

41. Which act was enacted to ensure parties involved in a real estate transaction receive complete settlement cost disclosure?

    A.   RESPA
    B.   FHA
    C.   Clean Water Act
    D.   Civil Rights Act

42. What is the name given to the downward movement of water through soil?

    A.   Absorption
    B.   Filtration
    C.   Percolation
    D.   Proration

43. What type of income is generated by investing in a limited partnership?

    A.   Active income
    B.   Passive income
    C.   Surplus income
    D.   Savings

44. What mortgage type allows the mortgagor to make payments only on the interest accrued?

    A.   Blanket mortgage
    B.   Balloon mortgage
    C.   Graduated mortgage
    D.   Straight term mortgage

45. Mary's agent helped her purchase a property and negotiated a mortgage for her. This agent also represented the seller. What type of agent did Mary engage?

    A.   Single agent
    B.   Dual agent
    C.   Double agent
    D.   None of the above

46. What is the land survey process that involves the surveyor starting at an easily identifiable point and describing the property in terms of courses and distances and eventually returning to the starting point?

    A.   ALTA
    B.   Boundary construction
    C.   Metes and bounds
    D.   Topographic surveys

47. What arrangement allows the seller to absorb an existing loan in order to allow the buyer another mortgage?

    A.   Simple mortgage
    B.   Wraparound mortgage
    C.   Mortgage by conditional sale
    D.   Reverse mortgage

48. Which real estate participants are legally required to be licensed?

    A.   Sellers
    B.   Buyers
    C.   Lenders
    D.   Real estate agents and brokers

49. What is the term used to refer to the act of mixing money belonging to a client with one's own funds?

   A.   Commingling
   B.   Investing
   C.   Stealing
   D.   Saving

50. What is the effect of a larger money supply on the interest rates?

   A.   They decrease
   B.   They increase
   C.   Remains constant
   D.   They have no relationship

51. What is a homeowner's policy that covers two parts: property and liability?

   A.   HO1
   B.   HO2
   C.   HO3
   D.   HO4

52. What is the name given to tax calculated based on the value of an asset?

   A.   Ad valorem tax
   B.   Property tax
   C.   Capital gains tax
   D.   Transfer tax

53. What kind of lease agreement requires the landlord to pay for all expenses?

   A.   Gross lease
   B.   Ground lease
   C.   Net lease
   D.   Sublease

54. If a seller nets $442,000 from the sale of her home, and the commission is 5%, how much did the home sell for?

   A. $464,100
   B. $420,952
   C. $459,680
   D.   None of the above

55. What is the short-term loan that covers the interval between selling one property and buying another?

   A.   Bridge Loan
   B.   Cash flow
   C.   Cash on cash return
   D.   Mortgage

56. What are the set rules established for condominium or co-op tenants?

   A.   House rules
   B.   Investment agreement
   C.   Regulations
   D.   Policy

57. Who is responsible for the rent in a sublease?

   A. New tenant
   B. Lessee
   C. Lessor
   D. Roommate

58. What income type does a salary fall under?

   A. Active income
   B. Passive income
   C. Savings
   D. Investment

59. What is the name given to an estate that gives the holder temporary possession rights?

   A. Concurrent estates
   B. Estate for years
   C. Freehold estates
   D. Leasehold estate

60. What is a permit issued to a builder stating the property is fit for occupancy?

   A. Certificate of occupancy
   B. Contract of sale
   C. Landmark designation
   D. Receipt of sales deposit

61. What kind of mortgage pays off the principal?

   A. Amortized loan
   B. Fixed- rate loan
   C. Floating rate loan
   D. Mortgage

62. What is the income that is left after all operating costs are paid in a real estate investment?

   A. Investment
   B. Net operating income
   C. Profit
   D. Revenue

63. Which lease allows for changes in rent within the lease term?

   A. Graduated lease
   B. Lease break
   C. Sublease
   D. Value point

64. What is the married couple's capital gains tax exclusion on the sale of their primary home?

   A. $50,000
   B. $75,000
   C. $250,000
   D. $500,000

65. What should a licensee do with their pocket card?

A. Advertise it
B. Carry a physical copy or have a digital image on a device
C. File it
D. Use it to get clients

66. Besides the real estate agents, who is eligible for a license?

A. Attorney
B. Broker
C. Mortgage broker
D. Lender

67. What is a single person's capital gains tax exclusion?

A. $25,000
B. $100,000
C. $250,000
D. $500,000

68. What is the term given to violation of neighbor's property by trespassing?

A. Easement
B. Escheat
C. Encroachment
D. Encumbrance

69. What type of insurance is referred to as renters insurance?

A. HO1
B. HO2
C. HO3
D. HO4

70. What is a form of co-ownership by which all parties have undivided interests in the property but no right of survivorship?

A. Tenancy in common
B. Tenancy in entirety
C. Joint tenancy
D. Ownership in severalty

71. What conveys a grantor's interest in real property?

A. Deed
B. Insurance
C. Title
D. Warrant

72. What is the chain of deeds and other documents used in transferring title of land from one owner to another consecutively?

A. Abstract of title
B. Deed chain
C. History of deed
D. Chain of title

73. If you paid a down payment of $200,000 for a property worth $1,000,000 dollars and you currently rent it out for $4,000 a month, what is the cash on cash return?

    A.   4%
    B.   4.8%
    C.   20%
    D.   24%

74. What is a Certificate of Eligibility?

    A.   Certificate that shows one is to be exempt from property tax
    B.   Certificate that is presented by veterans to show proof that they have met the minimum service requirements to be eligible for a VA loan
    C.   Certificate that shows a construction is fit for occupancy
    D.   Certificate that shows merit

75. What is the insurance policy that protects a lender from loss due to disputes over ownership of a property and defects in the title?

    A.   Hazard insurance
    B.   Home warranty
    C.   Homeowner's insurance
    D.   Title insurance

76. Property that has a divided form of ownership is called?

    A.   Cooperative
    B.   Planned unit development
    C.   Time-share
    D.   Joint tenants

77. What is the definition of a syndication?

    A.   Income that is earned by a spouse prior to marriage
    B.   Land that is divided into smaller pieces of land
    C.   Mutual funds that invest in rental properties
    D.   Real estate that is purchased by a group which includes at least one sponsor and several investors

78. Which of the following is **not** an essential element of a contract?

    A.   Notarized signature
    B.   Consideration
    C.   Agreement by offer and acceptance
    D.   Competent parties

79. Which listing agreement allows the owner of the listed property to sell the property on their own and not have to pay commission to the listing broker?

    A.   Open listing
    B.   Option listing
    C.   Exclusive agency listing
    D.   Both A and C

80. What is the listing agreement that gives the broker the payment of commission no matter who sells the property?

    A.   Entirety
    B.   Exclusive-right-to-sell listing
    C.   Open listing
    D.   Net Listing

81. Which is an example of functional obsolescence?

    A. Four bedrooms and one bathroom in a private residence
    B. All bedrooms located on the 2nd floor and only one bathroom located on the 1st floor
    C. Walking through one bedroom to get to another bedroom
    D. All of the above

82. Which act was passed to protect consumers from being scammed when purchasing raw land?

    A. Interstate Land Sales Full Disclosure Act
    B. Federal Fair Housing Act
    C. Equal Credit Opportunity Act
    D. Federal Real Estate Law

83. Which statement is a listing agent required to reveal to a prospective buyer?

    A. The physical health of the previous owner
    B. Renovations made within the last 5 years
    C. Re-zoning of a property
    D. The number of members living in a home

84. Real estate taxes are based on the value of a home. A property owner can be taxed additionally to help pay for projects that benefit the neighborhood. What is this type of tax called?

    A. Property tax
    B. Special assessment tax
    C. Progressive tax
    D. Capital gains tax

85. Which anti-trust violation applies to real estate?

    A.   Monopolization
    B.   Price-fixing
    C.   Collusion
    D.   None of the above

THIS IS THE END OF THE NATIONAL PORTION.

STATE PORTION

1. _____ perform inspections of real property and are licensed by TREC.

   A. Appraisers
   B. Real estate salespersons
   C. Real estate inspectors
   D. Brokerages

2. What is an option fee?

   A. Money paid to a seller for the choice to terminate a real estate contract
   B. Money paid to a seller representing a good faith to buy a home
   C. Money paid to a broker for representing a buyer
   D. Money paid to a seller as good faith of home condition

3. The illegal act of when a fiduciary combines client money with their own funds is called _____.

   A. Principal
   B. Commingling
   C. Equity
   D. Ad valorem

4. An exclusive agency listing is an agreement that states that a seller agrees to pay a commission to the listing broker if _____.

   A. The broker brings in a buyer within 30 days
   B. The broker lists the property on MLS
   C. The broker sells the home for 10% higher than the property value
   D. The property is sold through the efforts of the real estate brokers

5. What does TRELA regulate?

    A. Code of ethics and standards of conduct
    B. License expiration and renewal
    C. Active license versus inactive license
    D. All of the above

6. What is the difference between a salesperson and a broker?

    A. There is no difference, they both do the same thing
    B. A salesperson owns the brokerage
    C. The broker works independently and a salesperson one works under a broker
    D. A salesperson directly contracts with clients

7. What is the purpose of the Texas Real Estate Commission?

    A. To provide a safeguard for consumers regarding real property transactions and valuation services
    B. To safeguard the rights of the licensed broker and salesperson
    C. To provide data regarding real estate transactions to the state government
    D. None of the above

8. Which survey system does Texas use?

    A. Public land survey system
    B. Meridian survey system
    C. Texas survey system
    D. Federal survey system

9. When must a real estate licensee disclose their license?

    A.   When they are applying for a mortgage
    B.   When they are action on behalf of a spouse, child or parent
    C.   When they own more than 10% of the business
    D.   Both B&C

10. How large are Municipal Utility Districts?

    A.   500 acres
    B.   They vary in size
    C.   100 acres
    D.   75 square miles

11. What kind of obsolescence occurs when there is a loss in value due to functional inadequacies of an improvement?

    A.   Economic obsolescence
    B.   Technological obsolescence
    C.   Function obsolescence
    D.   Legal obsolescence

12. Which form is required by Texas law and provides notice regarding brokerage services to prospective buyers, sellers, tenants and landlords?

    A.   Information about brokerage services form
    B.   Disclosure and statutory form
    C.   TREC brokerage transparency form
    D.   Consumer protection notice

13. Which of the following cannot be subpoenaed by TREC?

   A. Books
   B. Personal real property information
   C. Witnesses
   D. Records

14. Which of the following is true about a suspended real estate license?

   A. A suspended license cannot be reactivated until the licensee retakes the initial examination
   B. A person can get back their license when they pay back the money the recovery trust account paid out for claims against them
   C. A license cannot be suspended only revoked
   D. The licensee will be on a probationary period for 5 years

15. What are the TREC canons of professional ethics and conduct?

   A. A list of 4 rules adopted by TREC in the 1970's
   B. A list of state laws regarding real estate transactions passed in the 1990's
   C. A list of 5 standards for real estate licensees adopted by TREC
   D. Disciplinary action that can be enforced by TREC

16. The TREC consumer information form 1-1 applies to _____.

   A. Real estate licensees
   B. Appraisers
   C. Inspectors
   D. Both A&C

17. Property under the homestead exemption is not protected from foreclosure or certain debts. It is protected from _____.

A. Forced sale
B. Unpaid property taxes
C. Unpaid past-due child support
D. Missed mortgage payments

18. Which of the following conditions must a licensed inspector report because they are deemed as "deficient"?

A. An unlicensed property addition
B. Improperly installed, malfunction or missing ground fault circuit protection devices for garages, bathrooms, and other exterior areas
C. Improperly installed appliances and safety devices
D. Both B&C

19. _____ pertains to real property of a deceased person who fails to leave a will.

A. Community estate
B. Inheritance Laws
C. Laws of Descent and Distribution
D. Texas Estate Laws

20. Property sold to a buyer needed repairs which were not stated prior to or during closing. In order to hold the seller responsible for repairs a buyer must _____.

A. Have proof of the damaged properties
B. Find the damages within 30 days of the closing date
C. Have proof the selling agent knew of the damages
D. Prove that the seller withheld material facts regarding the home's condition

21. How does a broker terminate the sponsorship of a sales agent?

   A.   Provide written notice to the sales agent

   B.   Provide notice face to face to the sales agent and notify TREC

   C.   A broker cannot terminate the sponsorship

   D.   Notify TREC who will notify the sales agent

22. _____ is a form of ownership of property by more than one person.

   A.   Joint tenancy

   B.   Sole proprietary

   C.   Tenancy in common

   D.   Community property

23. Which legal concept allows a trespasser to gain legal title over property from the owner?

   A.   Jurisdiction

   B.   Land leaseback

   C.   Adverse possession

   D.   Nominal consideration

24. Which type of licensee does not have the authorization to practice in Texas but can collect a commission from a Texas broker.

   A.   Texas sales agent

   B.   Unlicensed broker

   C.   Foreign broker

   D.   None of the above

25. Texas provides buyers with a _____, which allows a buyer to terminate a deal within a certain amount of days.

    A. Option period
    B. Earnest money
    C. Option fee
    D. Grace period

26. What is the maximum penalty for violating the Texas Deceptive Trade Practices Act?

    A. $20,000 per violation
    B. $10,000 per violation
    C. The limit differs per case and has no max
    D. $20,000 for all violations

27. The Seller's Disclosure Act applies to the sale of residential property that has up to how many units?

    A. 1 unit
    B. 4 units
    C. 5 units
    D. 8 units

28. Which document states that a home has met all building codes and is suitable for occupancy?

    A. Certificate of reasonable value
    B. Certificate of eligibility
    C. Certificate of occupancy
    D. Usury

29. The salesman licensing education requires _____ hours.

    A.   180 hours
    B.   200 hours
    C.   300 hours
    D.   175 hours

30. The state of Texas requires all leases that are _____ to be in writing.

    A.   Less than 1 year
    B.   Longer than one year
    C.   All leases need to be in writing
    D.   5 years or longer

31. Which form is used to provide notice about flood hazard areas?

    A.   Information about special flood hazard areas
    B.   Addendum for coastal area property
    C.   Texas flood hazard form
    D.   None of the above

32. What is the definition of a gross lease?

    A.   A lease that states that the tenant is responsible for all operating expenses of the property
    B.   A lease that states the property is to be rented as is
    C.   A lease that states the landlord will pay the operating expenses of the property
    D.   A long-term lease that requires the tenant to pay all operating expenses

33. A broker is required to keep documents for 4 years. Which is not a document they are required to keep?

   A.   Property management agreement
   B.   Lease application forms
   C.   Move-in and move-out property condition forms
   D.   They are required to keep all the listed documents

34. What kind of depreciation occurs when a house is too close to a high traffic road?

   A.   Economic depreciation
   B.   Functional depreciation
   C.   Physical deterioration
   D.   Incurable depreciation

35. Which statement is true about a suspended broker's license?

   A.   The broker is allowed to complete all active listings but cannot take on new ones
   B.   The broker is automatically fired from their firm
   C.   The salesperson working under the broker must find a new sponsor to resume working
   D.   The salesperson working under the broker can take over the broker's listings

36. _____ is not recognized by the state of Texas but it is a form of concurrent ownership between a husband and a wife.

   A.   Tenancy by the entirety
   B.   Community property
   C.   Unity of possession
   D.   Unity of marriage

37. Texas Property Code chapter 221, also known as _____, governs and regulates timeshare interests.

    A. Texas Investment Property Act
    B. Texas Property Act
    C. Texas Timeshare and Vacation Property Act
    D. Texas Timeshare Act

38. What is a restrictive covenant?

    A. A contractual promise that states how a specified piece of property can be used
    B. An agreement on regarding the number of people allowed in a residential property
    C. A clause in a leasing agreement that states the percentage the rent can be raised
    D. The right the government has to acquire private property for public use

39. A loan that is issued to the buyer by the seller of the property as part of the property transaction is called a _____.

    A. Interest-only mortgage
    B. Purchase-money mortgage
    C. Fixed rate mortgage
    D. FHA loan

40. Which is not a type of concurrent estate in Texas?

    A. Joint tenancies
    B. Tenancies in common
    C. Life estate
    D. None of the above

THIS IS THE END OF THE STATE PORTION.

Answer Key – National Portion

1.	A	21.	C	41.	A	61.	A	81.	D
2.	A	22.	A	42.	C	62.	B	82.	A
3.	D	23.	C	43.	B	63.	A	83.	C
4.	D	24.	A	44.	D	64.	D	84.	B
5.	D	25.	B	45.	B	65.	B	85.	B
6.	A	26.	A	46.	C	66.	A		
7.	B	27.	B	47.	B	67.	C		
8.	C	28.	C	48.	D	68.	C		
9.	C	29.	C	49.	A	69.	D		
10.	B	30.	A	50.	A	70.	A		
11.	A	31.	B	51.	C	71.	A		
12.	D	32.	D	52.	A	72.	D		
13.	D	33.	B	53.	A	73.	D		
14.	C	34.	A	54.	D	74.	B		
15.	D	35.	C	55.	A	75.	D		
16.	B	36.	B	56.	A	76.	C		
17.	C	37.	A	57.	B	77.	D		
18.	B	38.	D	58.	A	78.	A		
19.	D	39.	B	59.	D	79.	D		
20.	A	40.	A	60.	A	80.	B		

1. **A) Pre-approval**

Prior to purchasing a property, the borrower can visit a lender and obtain a pre-approval letter stating the amount of credit the lender is willing to accord the buyer which will help determine what the buyer can afford.

2. **A) Usable Square Footage**

Usable square footage is the amount of space you actually occupy in a leased space.

3. **D) Principal**

The principal is the amount of money that a lender gives a borrower to facilitate property purchase. Payment of principal results in increase in borrower's equity.

4.   **D) VA mortgage**

This is a mortgage plan that is tailored to assist service members and their surviving spouses to become homeowners. There are usually a lot of qualifying standards put in place to be eligible for this type of mortgage and it is usually offered by banks and other credit facilities. The Veteran administration usually acts as a guarantor for the loan. Qualified Veterans are usually eligible for 100% financing.

5.   **D) Remaining term**

It is usually used to complete the period of time left on a loan and the amount of principal payment to be covered within that period.

6.   **A) Leaseback**

This is an arrangement that allows a seller to lease a property from the purchaser on transfer of ownership. The details surrounding the lease arrangement are usually discussed immediately after the sale.

7.   **B) Easement in gross**

Easement in gross is the agreement that attaches rights to the tenant over the property. Transfer of the land results in an immediate termination of the agreement. The agreement can be renegotiated with the new tenant over time.

8.   **C) Prepayment penalty**

This is the penalty placed on the significant payment of a mortgage within the first five years of the loan. This penalty exists to protect lenders from loss of interest income.

9.   **C) Private mortgage insurance**

These insurance payments are usually discontinued once a buyer builds up to 20% equity on the home.

10.   **B) Third party originator.**

This is any third party used to originate a loan. Lenders often employ the services of third-party moderators to underwrite and originate loans. They offer no ongoing and lasting responsibility for the mortgage.

11. **A) Capital Improvement**

This is the addition of a permanent change in a structure or restoration of damaged property. It is done to increase the longevity and market value of the property. For an item to be considered a capital investment, it has to be a permanent addition and capable of improving the value of the property.

12. **D) Transfer tax.**

This is any tax that is levied on transfer of ownership or title of property from one individual to another. It is usually non-deductible. It is usually levied at the local or federal level depending on the type of property changing ownership.

13. **D) All of the above**

Sales Comparison Approach, Cost Approach, and Income Approach are all appraisal methods.

14. **C) One year**

An asset must be held for at least one year before selling in order for profits to be categorized as long-term capital gains.

15. **D) All of the above**

Operating expenses include any costs associated with the operation and maintenance of an income-producing property.

16. **B) Refusing to leave a property despite expiration or termination of lease**

Commonly compared to an eviction, which is the legal removal of an individual from a lease due to violation of the terms of the agreement.

17. **C) Rate lock**

This occurs when lenders lock in a rate because it is the lowest rate being offered at the time. It is not a legally binding agreement and borrowers are allowed to abandon the rates based on the rising and falling.

18. **B) Lease option**

A lease option is a lease agreement that gives the tenant a choice to purchase the property within or at the end of the lease. It gives the buyer flexibility to make a purchase on the property. Usually involves an upfront agreement between the tenant and the landlord.

19. **D) The cooling capacity of an air conditioner and is measured in tons**

It is determined by measuring the size of the space being serviced by the air conditioner. The size area of the room is measured and multiplied by 25 BTU to determine the cooling capacity required in an air conditioner.

20. **A) Mortgage broker**

This is an individual that serves as an intermediate between lenders and brokers. A mortgage broker facilitates negotiations of interest rates and takes circulation of paperwork between the lender and the borrowers.

21. **C) $350,000**

$105,000 / 0.3 = $350,000

22. **A) Notice to cure**

This is a notice given to a leaseholder by the landlord regarding participation in activities that are not allowed in the building. The tenant is given 10 days to correct the mistake. Refusal to make adjustment results in the tenant being served a notice of termination.

23. **C) Pitch**

Defines the steepness of a roof. It is used to determine the material used for roofing and the space in the attic. It is also used to determine stability so that corrective measures can be undertaken early.

24. **A) The client**

A broker is required to work in the best interests of the client to ensure the best possible deal for the client.

25. **B) Easement**

This is the right to use another person's land temporarily without actually possessing it.

26. **A) Disabled**

Disabled, veterans, elderly, farmers, Gold Star Parents, and Star Program Homeowners. The above classes of people can get partial tax exemption by having the values of their homes reduced translating in reduced property taxes.

27. **B) 18 years**

This is the minimum required age for a real estate agent that has taken the education course and passed the qualifying exam.

28. **C) Fuse**

A fuse is a small conductor that is designed to melt under high current to break the circuit. A fuse should always maintain a series connection to the component of the circuit.

29. **C) A contract that involves both a promisor and promisee**

This contract occurs when both parties exchange a promise for a promise. Both parties enter into an agreement to fulfill their side of the bargain. Each party is also an obligor and obligee in this type of contract.

30. **A) Assessed value**

Assessed value is the monetary value assigned to a property and is usually used to determine the value of a property for the purpose of taxation.

31. **B) Environmental Protection Agency**

The Environmental Protection Agency is tasked with protecting both human and environmental health. The agency creates standards and laws promoting health of individuals and the environment and participates in upholding them by administering correcting efforts like CERCLA.

32. **D) Pro Forma Statement**

This is an estimate summary of income production if the current trends are maintained. This is usually in multifamily properties in order to help the investor understand general financial operations of the property.

33. **B) Create record of refusal in writing**

In the case where a client refuses to sign a disclosure, the agent is required to clearly state the names of the client and the facts surrounding the refusal to sign the disclosure. An agent is also required to sign a declaration in the presence of a notary public and have it notarized.

34. **A) Mortgage**

A voluntary lien is a claim a debtor has over the property of another and is initiated by the debtor as in the case of a mortgage. The debtor cannot legally sell the property as it is considered collateral.

35.   **C) Broker**

An agent resorts to a broker for commission as the law does not allow salespersons to work independently and therefore cannot be paid directly. A broker on receiving commission from the sale of the property is required to split the commission amongst the agents that were involved in the transaction.

36.   **B) Ownership in severalty**

This is a situation where real estate is owned by a single person or entity providing the owner with the most control of the land. A sole owner is at will to take any action on the land such as selling or leasing.

37.   **A) People who pose as real estate clients to check if fair housing is being practiced**

Testing was initiated under the Fair Housing Act to ensure that housing providers act in accordance with the fair housing laws that protect against discrimination based on race, origin and gender.

38.   **D) Accretion**

This is the natural growth of a parcel of land due to mother nature. It occurs due to accumulation of soil on the shoreline of a water body. A decrease due to erosion is also possible.

39.   **B) 27.5 years**

Depreciation is the loss of value of a property due to age, wear and tear. A residential property can only declare depreciation after 27.5 years in order to reduce the value of the property and property tax on the property.

40.   **A) Chattel**

A chattel is a tangible property which is either mobile or immobile. However, this term cannot be used to describe real estate holdings.

41.   **A) RESPA**

The Real Estate Settling Procedures Act was developed in order to protect the parties involved in a real estate transaction from abuse during the settlement process. The act mandates lenders and brokers to disclose all matters crucial to the transaction service, settlement service and consumer protection laws

42. **C) Percolation**

This is the process in which water reaches the subsoil and roots. The pore space present in soil acts as a medium for the water to percolate. The ability of water to move through soil is dependent on the soil texture and structure. Some soils allow water to move very deep into the ground which may result in mixing with underground water reservoirs.

43. **B) Passive income**

This is income that is generated with minimal activity. It requires little to no effort to earn on a daily basis.

44. **D) Straight term mortgage**

A straight term mortgage is a mortgage that allows the mortgagor to make monthly payments on the interest accrued throughout the mortgage's lifespan. The principal remains unpaid until a set date where it becomes due for payment in full.

45. **B) Dual agent**

Mary's agent was able to perform the above transactions for her because he was working for both the Mary and the seller of the property.

46. **C) Metes and bounds**

This is a legal principle of land description and uses natural and artificial landmarks as boundaries. It is often used to describe irregular tracts of land. Metes defines straight line distances while bounds defines a less regular but identifiable lines. Measurements from an original point that is a monument and metes and bounds are described taking into account the boundaries. The process is repeated until the surveyor returns to the original point.

47. **B) Wraparound mortgage**

Wraparound mortgages are used to refinance property. They are mini loans that include the balance of the preexisting mortgage and an additional loan to cover the new property. The seller is granted a promissory note highlighting the amount due.

48. **D) Real estate agents and brokers**

They need to be licensed as they legally represent clients, buyers and sellers, in transferring ownership of property.

49. **A) Commingling**

This is a breach of trust that occurs when a representative of a client mixes individual funds with that of the client making it impossible to determine the amounts that belong to each individual.

50. **A) They decrease**

Money supply is influenced by supply and demand. An increase in the money supply will result in a decreased interest rate making it easier to borrow and vice versa. Therefore, money and interest rates have an inversely proportional relationship.

51. **C) HO3**

A home owner's policy is a property insurance that covers losses and damages done to the insured's house and assets within the home. It also provides liability coverage against accidents within the home.

52. **A) Ad valorem tax**

This is the tax levied by a municipality or local government entity based on assessed value. A public assessor is engaged to value the property in order to calculate the tax owed.

53. **A) Gross lease**

This is a flat rent fee that included all expenses associated with ownership. It is inclusive of incidental charges such as taxes, insurance and utilities. It is an uncommon lease as landlords are unaware of the utility charges that may be incurred by a tenant.

54. **D) None of the above**

$442,000 / (1 - 0.05) = $465,263

55. **A) Bridge Loan**

This is a short-term loan of up to one year that provides cash flow enabling an individual to meet current obligations while awaiting permanent financing. It is often used in real estate to purchase a new home while awaiting the sale of the old property.

56. **A) House rules**

These are set rules that have been put in place to ensure the comfort of the tenants living within the building. Violation of the house rules clause may result in eviction.

57. **B) Lessee**

The original tenant for rent as he/she is liable to the owner. In case of overdue rent by the new tenant, the original tenant is held accountable.

58. **A) Active income**

This is an income earned from performing services. Active participation is required to yield payment.

59. **D) Leasehold estate**

This is a lease that allows the tenant to have real property for an extended period of time. A time frame is agreed upon in the lease and the tenant is allowed to erect structures and profit from the business that has been established at the site.

60. **A) Certificate of occupancy**

This is a legal statement issued by the building department clearing a building for occupancy on meeting the building codes and other laws that surround the construction of a residential or commercial building. It can be obtained when a new building is constructed or an old building is repurposed.

61. **A) Amortized loan**

An amortized loan is a loan with a scheduled payment over a period of time that pays off the interest and principal. An amortized loan payment schedule focuses on paying off the interest and progresses into the principal.

62. **B) Net operating income**

This is a method used to value the income generating properties. To obtain the value, all expenses incurred during operations is subtracted to the total income produced by the property. To get the true value produced by the property, revenues earned must be included.

63. **A) Graduated lease**

A graduated lease is an agreement between the landlord and tenant that allows for periodic adjustment of monthly payments based on the market value of the property. It stands to benefit the landlord over a long period of time.

64. **D) $500,000**

In accordance with the Taxpayers Relief Act, a married couple is eligible for exclusion from capital gain tax for profits of up to $500,000. This is provided the property sold is a primary residence, they have been living in it for at least 2 years.

65. **B) Carry a physical copy or have a digital image on a device**

A pocket card is a pocket-sized license identifying the holder as a licensed agent. It contains a photo, name and business address of the holder.

66. **A) Attorney**

This is licensed broker that engages the services of other agents with intentions of splitting commission paid on the sale of a property.

67. **C) $250,000**

According to the Taxpayers relief act, a single person is eligible for a capital gains tax exemption for profits of up to $250,000 on the sale of a primary home.

68. **C) Encroachment**

Encroachment is a violation of property rights that occurs when an individual chooses to ignore set boundaries. This can be by extending structure into the neighbor's land or illegally entering the neighbor's property.

69. **D) HO4**

This insurance is designed to protect the insured and belongings from the covered losses. It covers liability, personal property, additional living expenses and medical payments to others. The insurance covers against risks specified in the policy.

70. **A) Tenancy in common**

A tenancy in common is a legal agreement where two or more people with undivided rights own a property. Members of a tenancy in common are not mandated to have equal rights and can enter the agreement at any time. Members of a tenancy in common are free to leave their shares to a beneficiary.

71. **A) Deed**

This is a signed legal document that conveys interest of a property and is used in cases of transfer of property provided a set of conditions are met. For a deed to hold legal merit, it must be filed in a public record.

72. **D) Chain of title**

This is an official ownership record of a property. It is usually maintained from a centralized registry. It is used widely to protect lenders and buyers from losses occurring due to errors in the title report.

73. **D) 24%**

($4,000 * 12) / $200,000 = 0.24

74. **B) Certificate that is presented by veterans to show proof that they have met the minimum service requirements to be eligible for a VA loan**

The Certificate of Eligibility serves as proof of a veteran's military service and must be provided to lenders during the VA loan process

75. **D) Title insurance**

A title insurance is based on the indemnity clause. It is taken by a buyer to protect the lender from loss caused by unidentified defects in the title. It acts against traditional insurance by protecting clients against claims on a past occurrence

76. **C) Time-share**

Also called vacation ownership, a time-share is shared ownership of a property. This type of property is typically a vacation property i.e. a condominium in a resort area. The buyer typically purchases a certain period of time for the unit, typically one- to two-week periods.

77. **D) Real estate that is purchased by a group which includes at least one sponsor and several investors**

Syndication is a method investors can use to invest in properties. Investors pool their financial and intellectual resources together to invest in properties that they would not be able to invest in individually.

78. **A) Notarized signature**

A notarized signature is not necessary in a contract. A legal purpose, competent parties, offer and acceptance, consideration and consent are the essential elements of a contract.

79. **D) Both A and C**

Exclusive agency listing is an agreement between a real estate firm and seller which grants the firm the exclusive rights to sell the property but also allows the seller to sell the home without paying a commission to the listing agent. An open listing is a property listing using multiple real estate agents. This type of listing also allows an owner to list and sell the property without paying a commission to an agent.

80. **B) Exclusive-right-to-sell listing**

A legal agreement under which the seller agrees to pay a commission to the listing broker. The listing broker acts as the agent and is provided commission whether the property is sold through the listing broker, seller or anyone else. An exception occurs when the seller names one or more individuals/entities as exemptions in the listing agreement.

81. **D) All of the above**

Functional obsolescence occurs when an objects usefulness or desirability has been reduced because of an outdated design feature. They are features that cannot be easily fixed.

82. **A) Interstate Land Sales Full Disclosure Act**

Passed in 1968, this act protects against land scams by facilitating the regulation of interstate land sales. Developers need to register subdivisions that contain more than 100 or more nonexempt lots. They may also provide purchasers with a disclosure statement (property report) prior to a sale.

83. **C) Re-zoning of a property**

A seller is required to disclose all known material facts regarding the property to a buyer. Personal information about the family is not required but a re-zoning of the property must be disclosed.

84. **B) Special assessment tax**

Property owners are sometimes taxed for improvements that effect some of the property owners within a taxing district. Only the property owners who have been affected will be taxed. These taxes pay for local infrastructure projects such as sewer lines, or construction and maintenance of roads.

85. **B) Price-fixing**

Price-fixing, boycotting and allocation of customer or markets are the most common anti-trust violations in real estate.

Answer Key – State Portion

1.	C	21.	A
2.	A	22.	A
3.	B	23.	C
4.	D	24.	C
5.	D	25.	A
6.	C	26.	B
7.	A	27.	B
8.	C	28.	C
9.	D	29.	A
10.	B	30.	B
11.	C	31.	A
12.	A	32.	C
13.	B	33.	D
14.	B	34.	D
15.	C	35.	C
16.	D	36.	A
17.	A	37.	D
18.	D	38.	A
19.	C	39.	B
20.	D	40.	C

1. **C) Real estate inspectors**

Inspectors inspect properties as part of a real estate transaction. They are required to used TREC standard report forms and provide information on the performance of certain systems which are part of the property.

2. **A) Money paid to a seller for the choice to terminate a real estate contract**

This gives a buyer the option to terminate a contract and should not be confused with earnest money. The option fee needs to be paid within 3 days of the effective contract and is most commonly used in Texas real estate transactions.

3. **B) Commingling**

A commingling makes it difficult to determine which funds belong to the fiduciary and which belong to the client.

4. **D) The property is sold through the efforts of the real estate broker**

    This agreement only pays commission to the broker if they sells the property. If the property is sold through the efforts of the seller, then the seller does not need to pay a commission to the listing broker.

5. **D) All of the above**

    TRELA regulate many things regarding Texas real estate from education, license requirements and client complaints.

6. **C) The brokerage works independently, and a salesperson only works under a broker**

    A broker is a managing agent of the brokerage and can work independently while a salesperson cannot. The license requirements and level of interaction differ between a salesperson and broker.

7. **A) To provide a safeguard for consumers regarding real property transactions and valuation services**

    TREC was established in 1949 by the Texas Legislature. It oversees real estate brokerage, property appraisals, home warranties, inspections, right-of-way services and timeshares. It also provides licensing, complaint investigation services, education and regulation services.

8. **C) Texas survey system**

    This system is based on Spanish land grants. It is split into 12 railroad districts that follow the county lines. There are 3 layers of this survey systems the Texas RRC district layer, Texas bay tracts layer and Texas land survey layer.

9. **D) Both B&C**

    Texas law states the licensee must disclose their license when they are representing themselves, a spouse, child or parent or when they are a trustee of a beneficiary who is their spouse, child or parent. They must also disclose their license when they own more than 10% of a business entity.

10. **B) They vary in size**

    The MUD vary in size but typically serve communities of a few hundred households. Texas has over 1,200 special district and most are outside of city limits.

11. **C) Functional obsolescence**

This occurs when there is a decrease in usefulness or desirability in real property due to an outdated design feature. There are two types of functional obsolescence, the super adequacy and deficiency.

12. **A) Information about brokerage services form**

This form is required at the first substantive communication and is the required method of providing information to buyers, sellers, tenants, and landlords. The form must be completely filled out and provided to the party and must be posted on the homepage of the business website.

13. **B) Personal real property information**

Books, witnesses and records can be subpoenaed by TREC. If the licensee does not produce the above, TREC can file a suit with the AG.

14. **B) A person can get back their license when they pay back the money the recovery trust account paid out for claims against them**

If TREC had to pay a claim out of the recovery trust account, then a licensee will not get their license back until they pay back the claim to the trust account.

15. **C) A list of 5 standards for real estate licensees adopted by TREC**

These canons of ethics that must be followed by real estate licensees. These canons were adopted by TREC in the 1970's and 1990's.

16. **D) Both A&C**

The consumer information form 1-1 applies to both licensees and inspectors. This form must be displayed in the broker's office.

17. **A) Forced sale**

The homestead exemption protects from forced sales to satisfy creditors i.e. payday lenders and debt collectors. It does not protect from defaulted second liens from home equity lines of credit and loans, unpaid IRS liens, past due child support, property taxes, government student loans and mortgage payments.

18. **D) Both B&C**

These deficiencies must be reported by the licensed inspector. Other deficiencies are malfunctioning carbon monoxide alarms and fire safety features i.e. smoke alarms, and lack of electrical bonding, ground and bonding on gas piping.

19. **C) Law of descent and distribution**

This law sets forth who is entitled to the estate of a person who has died without a will. It sets forth the right and liabilities of next of kin and heirs who are entitles to a share of the deceased person's property.

20. **D) Prove that the seller withheld material facts regarding the home's condition**

The buyer needs to prove that the seller withheld information about the home's condition. It is unlikely the seller will be held liable for repairs after escrow closes, especially if the seller disclosed known defects to the buyer

21. **A) Provide written notice to the sales agent**

The broker must provide notice to the sales agent in writing, return the license to TREC and notify the commission of the termination

22. **A) Joint tenancy**

Property ownership by two or more people where the tenants have the same interest. If a tenant dies, the share passes to the other owner(s).

23. **C) Adverse possession**

Adverse possession is controlled by statutes which has been passed by the state legislature. Whoever holds the legal title is the owner, unless the adverse possessor can prove otherwise.

24. **C) Foreign broker**

A broker who is licensed in another state or another country, does not have the right to practice in Texas, but they can receive a commission from a licensed Texas broker. The foreign broker's license needs to be active.

25. **A) Option period**

Option periods are typically 7-10 business days and allow the buyer to back out of a deal for any given reason without losing their earnest money.

26. **B) $10,000 per violation**

The DPTA has a maximum penalty of $10,000 per violation, which was reduced from $20,000 per violation in 2019. This was done to decrease abuse of the act.

27. **B) 4 units**

This act applies to the sale of residential property between 1 and 4 units, but sellers such as foreclosing lenders, bankruptcy trustees and estates are exempt. Sellers who have never lived in a home are not exempt from the Seller's Disclosure Act.

28. **C) Certificate of occupancy**

A building department or local government agency provides this certificate to certify that it complies with the county's building codes. A certificate is needed when a new building is built, property is changing from one use to another or a change of ownership.

29. **A) 180 hours**

180 hours of education is required for salesman licensing. It is 60 hours of principles in real estate, 30 hours in law agency, 30 hours in law of contracts, 30 hours in finance and 30 hours in promulgated contracts.

30. **B) Longer than one year**

The statute of frauds requires all leases that are more than one year to be in writing.

31. **A) Information about special flood hazard areas**

This form is used to provide notice to buyers about special flood hazard areas. It provide information about flood risk areas and flood insurance.

32. **C) A lease that states the landlord will pay the operating expenses of the property**

This type of leases states that even though the tenant is paying rent, the tenant is not responsible for maintaining the repairs or expenses. The landlord is responsible for paying for all expenses.

33. **D) They are required to keep all the listed documents**

According to TREC regulations a broker is required to keep all of the listed documents for 4 years.

34. **D) Incurable depreciation**

This type of depreciation is impossible to cure or is too expensive to be considered worth curing. A problem that causes more money to fix than its value does not make economic sense to repair.

35.   **C) The salesperson working under the broker must find a new sponsor to resume working**

The salesperson's license goes inactive until the salesperson finds a new sponsor to work under. They cannot perform any of the duties of the salesperson until they have found a new sponsor.

36.   **A) Tenancy by the entirety**

Not recognized in Texas, tenancy by the entirety only lasts as long as the couple is married. It states that each party has the right to survivorship over property and cannot be terminated without consent by the other.

37.   **D) Texas Timeshare Act**

This act governs and regulates timeshare interests which are comprised of properties and estates. This act only applies to properties that are located in the state of Texas.

38.   **A) A contractual promise that states how a specified piece of property can be used**

In Texas the restrictive covenant specifies any constraints on a piece of property. I.e. A homeowners deed states that a specific piece of land can only be used for single-family residential purposes.

39.   **B) Purchase-money mortgage**

This type of loan is also known as an owner or seller financing. The seller takes the role of the bank and offers the money to buy the home.

40.   **C) Life estate**

Joint tenancies and tenancies in common are forms of concurrent estate in Texas and are the most common.

Practice Test 4

Directions:

1. You have a 150-minute time limit for the national portion, and a 90-minute time limit for the state portion.

2. To pass, you must answer at least 56 out of 85 questions correctly on the national portion **AND** at least 21 out of 40 questions on the state portion.

3. Some questions will require mathematics. You may use a calculator.

4. **Phones and pagers are not allowed. Having either will result in automatic dismissal from the exam and nullification of exam scores.**

Tips:

- Answer all questions even if you are unsure.
- Mark any questions you are stuck on and revisit them after you are done. The exam is timed so make sure you finish as many questions as you can.
- After reading the question, try answering it in your head first to avoid getting confused by the choices.
- Read the entire question before looking at the answers.
- Use the process of elimination to filter out choices that don't seem correct to increase your chances of selecting the correct answer.
- Be aware of important keywords like **not, sometimes, always,** and **never**. These words completely alter the ask of the question so it's important to keep track of them.

PLEASE READ THESE INSTRUCTIONS CAREFULLY.

Name: _____   Date: _____

NATIONAL PORTION

1. Ⓐ Ⓑ Ⓒ Ⓓ	31. Ⓐ Ⓑ Ⓒ Ⓓ	61. Ⓐ Ⓑ Ⓒ Ⓓ
2. Ⓐ Ⓑ Ⓒ Ⓓ	32. Ⓐ Ⓑ Ⓒ Ⓓ	62. Ⓐ Ⓑ Ⓒ Ⓓ
3. Ⓐ Ⓑ Ⓒ Ⓓ	33. Ⓐ Ⓑ Ⓒ Ⓓ	63. Ⓐ Ⓑ Ⓒ Ⓓ
4. Ⓐ Ⓑ Ⓒ Ⓓ	34. Ⓐ Ⓑ Ⓒ Ⓓ	64. Ⓐ Ⓑ Ⓒ Ⓓ
5. Ⓐ Ⓑ Ⓒ Ⓓ	35. Ⓐ Ⓑ Ⓒ Ⓓ	65. Ⓐ Ⓑ Ⓒ Ⓓ
6. Ⓐ Ⓑ Ⓒ Ⓓ	36. Ⓐ Ⓑ Ⓒ Ⓓ	66. Ⓐ Ⓑ Ⓒ Ⓓ
7. Ⓐ Ⓑ Ⓒ Ⓓ	37. Ⓐ Ⓑ Ⓒ Ⓓ	67. Ⓐ Ⓑ Ⓒ Ⓓ
8. Ⓐ Ⓑ Ⓒ Ⓓ	38. Ⓐ Ⓑ Ⓒ Ⓓ	68. Ⓐ Ⓑ Ⓒ Ⓓ
9. Ⓐ Ⓑ Ⓒ Ⓓ	39. Ⓐ Ⓑ Ⓒ Ⓓ	69. Ⓐ Ⓑ Ⓒ Ⓓ
10. Ⓐ Ⓑ Ⓒ Ⓓ	40. Ⓐ Ⓑ Ⓒ Ⓓ	70. Ⓐ Ⓑ Ⓒ Ⓓ
11. Ⓐ Ⓑ Ⓒ Ⓓ	41. Ⓐ Ⓑ Ⓒ Ⓓ	71. Ⓐ Ⓑ Ⓒ Ⓓ
12. Ⓐ Ⓑ Ⓒ Ⓓ	42. Ⓐ Ⓑ Ⓒ Ⓓ	72. Ⓐ Ⓑ Ⓒ Ⓓ
13. Ⓐ Ⓑ Ⓒ Ⓓ	43. Ⓐ Ⓑ Ⓒ Ⓓ	73. Ⓐ Ⓑ Ⓒ Ⓓ
14. Ⓐ Ⓑ Ⓒ Ⓓ	44. Ⓐ Ⓑ Ⓒ Ⓓ	74. Ⓐ Ⓑ Ⓒ Ⓓ
15. Ⓐ Ⓑ Ⓒ Ⓓ	45. Ⓐ Ⓑ Ⓒ Ⓓ	75. Ⓐ Ⓑ Ⓒ Ⓓ
16. Ⓐ Ⓑ Ⓒ Ⓓ	46. Ⓐ Ⓑ Ⓒ Ⓓ	76. Ⓐ Ⓑ Ⓒ Ⓓ
17 Ⓐ Ⓑ Ⓒ Ⓓ	47. Ⓐ Ⓑ Ⓒ Ⓓ	77. Ⓐ Ⓑ Ⓒ Ⓓ
18. Ⓐ Ⓑ Ⓒ Ⓓ	48. Ⓐ Ⓑ Ⓒ Ⓓ	78. Ⓐ Ⓑ Ⓒ Ⓓ
19. Ⓐ Ⓑ Ⓒ Ⓓ	49. Ⓐ Ⓑ Ⓒ Ⓓ	79. Ⓐ Ⓑ Ⓒ Ⓓ
20. Ⓐ Ⓑ Ⓒ Ⓓ	50. Ⓐ Ⓑ Ⓒ Ⓓ	80. Ⓐ Ⓑ Ⓒ Ⓓ
21. Ⓐ Ⓑ Ⓒ Ⓓ	51. Ⓐ Ⓑ Ⓒ Ⓓ	81. Ⓐ Ⓑ Ⓒ Ⓓ
22. Ⓐ Ⓑ Ⓒ Ⓓ	52. Ⓐ Ⓑ Ⓒ Ⓓ	82. Ⓐ Ⓑ Ⓒ Ⓓ
23. Ⓐ Ⓑ Ⓒ Ⓓ	53. Ⓐ Ⓑ Ⓒ Ⓓ	83. Ⓐ Ⓑ Ⓒ Ⓓ
24. Ⓐ Ⓑ Ⓒ Ⓓ	54. Ⓐ Ⓑ Ⓒ Ⓓ	84. Ⓐ Ⓑ Ⓒ Ⓓ
25. Ⓐ Ⓑ Ⓒ Ⓓ	55. Ⓐ Ⓑ Ⓒ Ⓓ	85. Ⓐ Ⓑ Ⓒ Ⓓ
26. Ⓐ Ⓑ Ⓒ Ⓓ	56. Ⓐ Ⓑ Ⓒ Ⓓ	
27. Ⓐ Ⓑ Ⓒ Ⓓ	57. Ⓐ Ⓑ Ⓒ Ⓓ	
28. Ⓐ Ⓑ Ⓒ Ⓓ	58. Ⓐ Ⓑ Ⓒ Ⓓ	
29. Ⓐ Ⓑ Ⓒ Ⓓ	59. Ⓐ Ⓑ Ⓒ Ⓓ	
30. Ⓐ Ⓑ Ⓒ Ⓓ	60. Ⓐ Ⓑ Ⓒ Ⓓ	

Name: _____   Date: _____

STATE PORTION

1.	Ⓐ Ⓑ Ⓒ Ⓓ	31.	Ⓐ Ⓑ Ⓒ Ⓓ
2.	Ⓐ Ⓑ Ⓒ Ⓓ	32.	Ⓐ Ⓑ Ⓒ Ⓓ
3.	Ⓐ Ⓑ Ⓒ Ⓓ	33.	Ⓐ Ⓑ Ⓒ Ⓓ
4.	Ⓐ Ⓑ Ⓒ Ⓓ	34.	Ⓐ Ⓑ Ⓒ Ⓓ
5.	Ⓐ Ⓑ Ⓒ Ⓓ	35.	Ⓐ Ⓑ Ⓒ Ⓓ
6.	Ⓐ Ⓑ Ⓒ Ⓓ	36.	Ⓐ Ⓑ Ⓒ Ⓓ
7.	Ⓐ Ⓑ Ⓒ Ⓓ	37.	Ⓐ Ⓑ Ⓒ Ⓓ
8.	Ⓐ Ⓑ Ⓒ Ⓓ	38.	Ⓐ Ⓑ Ⓒ Ⓓ
9.	Ⓐ Ⓑ Ⓒ Ⓓ	39.	Ⓐ Ⓑ Ⓒ Ⓓ
10.	Ⓐ Ⓑ Ⓒ Ⓓ	40.	Ⓐ Ⓑ Ⓒ Ⓓ
11.	Ⓐ Ⓑ Ⓒ Ⓓ		
12.	Ⓐ Ⓑ Ⓒ Ⓓ		
13.	Ⓐ Ⓑ Ⓒ Ⓓ		
14.	Ⓐ Ⓑ Ⓒ Ⓓ		
15.	Ⓐ Ⓑ Ⓒ Ⓓ		
16.	Ⓐ Ⓑ Ⓒ Ⓓ		
17	Ⓐ Ⓑ Ⓒ Ⓓ		
18.	Ⓐ Ⓑ Ⓒ Ⓓ		
19.	Ⓐ Ⓑ Ⓒ Ⓓ		
20.	Ⓐ Ⓑ Ⓒ Ⓓ		
21.	Ⓐ Ⓑ Ⓒ Ⓓ		
22.	Ⓐ Ⓑ Ⓒ Ⓓ		
23.	Ⓐ Ⓑ Ⓒ Ⓓ		
24.	Ⓐ Ⓑ Ⓒ Ⓓ		
25.	Ⓐ Ⓑ Ⓒ Ⓓ		
26.	Ⓐ Ⓑ Ⓒ Ⓓ		
27.	Ⓐ Ⓑ Ⓒ Ⓓ		
28.	Ⓐ Ⓑ Ⓒ Ⓓ		
29.	Ⓐ Ⓑ Ⓒ Ⓓ		
30.	Ⓐ Ⓑ Ⓒ Ⓓ		

NATIONAL PORTION

1. Which of the following is considered commercial real estate?

   A. Office building
   B. Warehouse
   C. Multifamily house
   D. All of the above

2. Jack is trying to convince Mary to move to a particular neighborhood because the residents there are of her ethnic background and religion. What is guilty of?

   A. Blockbusting
   B. Discriminating
   C. Convincing
   D. Steering

3. What type of lease would a tenant take when using a warehouse for the purpose of manufacturing and distribution?

   A. Gross lease
   B. Net lease
   C. Percentage lease
   D. Proprietary lease

4. What is a notice given on a pending lawsuit?

   A. Lis Pendens
   B. Statute of limitations
   C. Notice of intent
   D. Notice of default

5. Who issues variances?

   A. Architectural Review Board
   B. EPA
   C. Municipal Engineers
   D. Zoning Board of Appeals

6. What is the name given to an individual who originates, sells and services mortgage loans?

   A. Mortgage Banker
   B. Mortgage Broker
   C. Lender
   D. Borrower

7. What is the exterior layer of a house?

   A. Eaves
   B. Flashing
   C. Pitch
   D. Sheathing

8. Who holds on to the security deposit?

   A. Agent
   B. Broker
   C. Buyer
   D. Landlord

9. What is the term used to define the estimated age of a property based on its utilities and physical wear and tear?

   A. Economic life
   B. Effective age
   C. Use discount
   D. Depreciation

10. How long are brokers required to hold on to property files?

    A. One year
    B. Three years
    C. Five years
    D. Never

11. What is the unit used to measure furnace or air conditioner capacity?

    A. British Thermal Unit
    B. Bytes
    C. Joules
    D. Watts

12. What describes the type of estate granted within a lease?

    A. Acceleration clause
    B. Annuity law
    C. Cancellation clause
    D. Habendum clause

13. What type of income is income generated from a rental property?

    A. Active
    B. Passive
    C. Portfolio
    D. All the above

14. What is another name used to refer to land lease?

    A. Ground lease
    B. Home lease
    C. Percentage lease
    D. Estate lease

15. Which regulations govern the construction details of buildings with the sole interest of safeguarding the occupants and general public?

    A. APR
    B. Building codes
    C. Leasing laws
    D. Zoning codes

16. If a seller nets $325,000 from the sale of her home, and the commission is 3%, how much did the home sell for?

    A. $334,750
    B. $335,051
    C. $315,250
    D. $334,027

17. Personal property that is attached to real property, such as a chandelier, is regarded as

A. An emblement
B. An appliance
C. A fixture
D. A liability

18. What are outside amenities that maximize use of property called?

A. Cosmetic improvements
B. Essential improvements
C. Offsite improvements
D. Supplemental improvements

19. Which form of ownership passes the shares of ownership upon death?

A. Life estate
B. Severalty
C. Tenancy in common
D. Joint tenancy

20. If a property manager is fixing a leaky pipe, what type of maintenance is he doing?

A. Aesthetic maintenance
B. Appreciation
C. Breakdown prevention
D. Preventive maintenance

21. Which act was enacted in order to identify hazardous sites?

A. Americans with disabilities Act
B. CERCLA
C. Fair Housing Act
D. Civil Rights Act

22. What is tenancy in common?

A. A shared tenancy in which each holder has a distinct, separately transferable interest
B. A tenancy in which each holder has equal interest, where interest is automatically passed in case of death
C. A tenancy in which interest is returned to the public upon death
D. A tenancy in which a single owner owns full ownership of a property

23. What is the money available after deducting all expenses?

A. Cash out returns
B. Cash flow
C. Cash on cash return
D. Revenue

24. What is an involuntary lien?

A. A lien that arises without the property owner's consent
B. A lien that is initiated with owner's consent
C. A lien that cannot be cashed on
D. None of the above

25. What is the name given to property that legally qualifies as owner's principal property?

    A.   Commercial property
    B.   Homestead property
    C.   Real property
    D.   Personal property

26. A person authorized to handle a principal's affairs in one specific area is referred to as?

    A.   General agent
    B.   Dual agent
    C.   Multi agent
    D.   Special agent

27. What are real property rights conferred with ownership?

    A.   Bundle of rights
    B.   Right of first refusal
    C.   Riparian rights
    D.   Doctrine of equitable conversion

28. What is the fine placed for a violation of license law?

    A. $1,000
    B. $5,000
    C. $6,000
    D. $10,000

29. What is the term for commercial property depreciation?

    A.   5 years
    B.   29 years
    C.   39 years
    D.   40 years

30. The division of expenses at the time of closing between the buyer and seller in proportion to the actual use of a property is called?

    A.   Bill of sale
    B.   Loan to value ratio
    C.   Proration
    D.   Tax abatement

31. What is the equivalent of 1 cubic foot?

    A.   5.25 gallons
    B.   7.26 gallons
    C.   7.48 gallons
    D.   10 gallons

32. What is a statement that shows total revenues generated based on rent rolls and management styles?

    A.   Invoice statement
    B.   Income statement
    C.   Pro forma statement
    D.   Operating statement

33. What type of building is divided into two condominiums where the first is the co-op residential units (80%) and the second is for professional/commercial units (20%)?

    A. Condo
    B. Condop
    C. Co-op
    D. Multi family home

34. A person authorized to handle a principal's affairs in more than one specific area is referred to as?

    A. Special agent
    B. General Agent
    C. Dual agent
    D. Broker

35. What are the laws that limit the maximum interest rate that can be charged?

    A. APR
    B. Annuity laws
    C. FHA
    D. Usury

36. What is the nature of the title in co-op ownership?

    A. Freehold
    B. Leasehold
    C. Regular hold
    D. Lease assignment

37. What is a non-possessory interest in property giving a lienholder the right to foreclose?

    A. Mortgage
    B. Duties
    C. Taxes
    D. Revenue

38. What is the agreement that allows the tenant to continue living on a property once the lease has expired?

    A. Tenancy in common
    B. Tenancy in entirety
    C. Tenancy in sufferance
    D. Ownership in severalty

39. Can a salesperson hold other jobs?

    A. Yes
    B. No
    C. Only if it is in real estate
    D. Maybe

40. What does the Secondary Mortgage Market refer to in the loan process?

    A. Buyers that buy houses on mortgage
    B. Sellers that offer buy down arrangement
    C. Lending market
    D. Private investors and government agencies that buy and sell real estate mortgages

41. What are air rights?

    A.   Right to breath
    B.   Right to own an airspace
    C.   Right to package air
    D.   Rights granted to a property owner on the vertical space above the property

42. What is the relationship where agents work together in the best interest of their respective clients?

    A.   Dual agency
    B.   Single agency
    C.   Co-broking
    D.   Co-borrowing

43. What is the legal term for passing responsibility of your apartment onto another tenant?

    A.   Sub lease
    B.   Lease assignment
    C.   Leasehold
    D.   Lease break

44. If you have a loan of $200,000 with a 12% interest, how much do you pay in interest every month?

    A. $1,200
    B. $2,000
    C. $2,400
    D. $24,000

45. What are the extra charges above the selling costs that are incurred by the buyer on the purchase of a home?

    A.   Common costs
    B.   Closing costs
    C.   Down payment
    D.   Short fall

46. What are the monthly charges imposed on condo tenants?

    A.   Common charges
    B.   Common costs
    C.   Service fees
    D.   Short fall

47. What is the name given to the ratio defined by dividing monthly debt payments to gross monthly income?

    A.   Loan to value ratio
    B.   Debt to income ratio
    C.   Earnest money deposit
    D.   Foreclosure

48. What is the percentage amount of the selling price that is deposited by the buyer when closing a real estate transaction?

    A.   Down payment
    B.   Escrow
    C.   Earnest money deposit
    D.   Tax abatement

49. What is earnest money deposit?

    A. Money deposited by the buyer to the seller to show interest in the purchase of a home
    B. Purchase money
    C. Down payment
    D. Security deposit

50. What is the financial agreement that allows a third party to regulate payment where two parties are involved?

    A. Security deposit
    B. Sales deposit
    C. Escrow
    D. Earnest money deposit

51. What is the notice given when a tenant is in violation of the lease agreement and is up for eviction?

    A. Notice to cure
    B. Notice of intention
    C. Notice of termination
    D. Notice to quit

52. What is the notice given when a squatter is accommodated without the landlord's consent?

    A. Notice of default
    B. Notice of intention
    C. Notice to cure
    D. Notice to quit

53. What is the notice given to state that no work has been performed?

    A. Notice of cessation
    B. Notice given to evict an unruly tenant
    C. Notice filed in court by a lender on defaulting of payment
    D. Notice to discontinue the breach of lease within 10 days

54. What is the name given to a visit made to a potential property to identify the condition of the house?

    A. Final walk through
    B. Home inspection
    C. Appraisal
    D. Assessment

55. What mortgage plan allows a borrower to switch to a fixed-rate mortgage?

    A. Adjustable Rate Mortgage
    B. Convertible ARM
    C. Fixed rate mortgage
    D. Floating rate mortgage

56. What is the situation that arises when an individual that is legally required to make payments does not fulfill this obligation?

    A. Delinquency
    B. Defaulting
    C. Escalation clause
    D. Foreclosure

57. Which agency insures FHA-approved lenders?

    A.   CERCLA
    B.   Consumer Financial Protection Bureau
    C.   Federal Emergency Management Agency
    D.   Federal Housing Administration

58. Which agency is commissioned with overseeing products and services offered to consumers in the finance industry?

    A.   Consumer Financial Protection Bureau
    B.   Federal Housing Administration
    C.   Environmental Protection Agency
    D.   Federal Emergency Management Agency

59. What service allows brokers to share their listings?

    A.   Broker Listing Service
    B.   Single Agency Listing
    C.   Multiple Listing Service
    D.   Shared Listing Service

60. What is the contract covering household maintenance systems?

    A.   Deed
    B.   Home warranty
    C.   Hazard insurance
    D.   HO4

61. What is the name given to a real estate transaction where buyers outbid each other for the property?

    A.   Acceleration clause
    B.   Escalation clause
    C.   Public auction
    D.   Tender

62. What is the name given to a notice given showing interest in a property?

    A.   Notice of cessation
    B.   Notice to cure
    C.   Notice of default
    D.   Notice of intent

63. What is the increase in the value of a property?

    A.   Appreciation
    B.   Depreciation
    C.   Obsolescence
    D.   All of the above

64. What is the mortgage payment plan that involves making payments every fortnight?

    A.   Balloon mortgage
    B.   Biweekly mortgage
    C.   Blanket mortgage
    D.   Graduated mortgage

65. What term is used to describe the document attached to an original contract?

A. Addendum
B. Signed agreement
C. Requirements clause
D. Terms and conditions

66. What refinancing method allows a borrower to acquire cash from the transaction?

A. Cash flow
B. Cash out refinance
C. Cash on cash return
D. Refinancing

67. Who oversees that code restrictions are followed and construction / renovation are done by licensed professionals?

A. Contractor
B. Department of Buildings
C. Zoning board
D. Architectural Review Board

68. What is the final stage of a real estate transaction?

A. Closing
B. Sale
C. Final walk through
D. Handing of the title

69. What is the percentage of the selling price that is usually earned by a real estate agent for facilitating the transaction?

A. Bonus
B. Commission
C. Salary
D. Rent

70. What is the name of fees paid to the lender at closing in exchange for a reduced interest rate?

A. Mortgage
B. Service fee
C. Discount points
D. Principal fee

71. Which Act was passed to protect against discrimination in borrowing?

A. Equal Credit Opportunity Act
B. Fair and Accurate Credit Transaction Act of 2003
C. The Fair Credit Reporting Act
D. Truth in Lending Act

72. What does the phrase "For Sale by Owner" mean?

A. A sale is being facilitated by an agent
B. Investors are open to receiving offers
C. A property sale is being handled without a real estate agent
D. All of the above

73. What is the name of the document used to summarize all the fees incurred by the lender and borrower during settlement of a loan?

    A. Financial statement
    B. Invoice
    C. IOU
    D. Settlement statement

74. Which entity determines the assessed value of a property?

    A. Building Inspector
    B. Municipal council
    C. Real estate agent
    D. Tax assessor

75. If a property is taxed at 40% with a tax levy of $88,000, what is its assessed value?

    A. $220,000
    B. $146,666
    C. $123,200
    D. None of the above

76. Which type of estate has rights to the property for an indefinite duration?

    A. List estate
    B. Estate for years
    C. Freehold estate
    D. Less-than-freehold estate

77. Which of the following is **not** an essential element of a deed?

    A. Signature of the grantee
    B. Date
    C. Identification of the grantor and grantee
    D. Adequate description of the property

78. What is a lessor?

    A. A person who leases real estate property from the owner of said property
    B. A person that makes a grant
    C. The owner of real estate who leases the property to another
    D. The person who transfers property by sale

79. What is the definition of a joint tenancy?

    A. When property is held by two or more parties
    B. When a third party trust owns the property
    C. When the seller and the buyer both own the property
    D. When the property is inherited by a family member

80. What is the definition of a trust deed?

    A. The owner of the real estate property who leases the property to another
    B. A deed with limited or no warranties
    C. A deed that transfers property to a family member
    D. A document used when one party has taken out a loan from another party to purchase property

81. _____ refers to land and buildings that need to be held for a long period of time to pay for themselves.

   A. Fixity
   B. Nonhomogeneity
   C. Situs
   D. Datum

82. A shop owner leases a space in a strip mall for 2 years. The strip mall is sold to a new owner during the duration of the lease. What is the status of the lease?

   A. The lease is void
   B. The new property owner and tenant must honor all the terms of the original lease
   C. The new property owner has the right to make changes to the lease within 30 days of the sale
   D. The lease starts fresh with the new property owner as the landlord

83. A homeowner's association does not allow owners to have pets. This is an example of a _____ clause.

   A. Possessions
   B. Contingency
   C. Restricted covenants
   D. Defeasance

84. Tenancy by the entirety is only applicable to _____.

   A. Homeowners with an FHA loan
   B. Low income homeowners
   C. Recently divorced couples
   D. Married couples

85. A building inspector must provide a(an) _____ before the property can be used.

A. Certificate of occupancy
B. Quitclaim deed
C. Pre-qualification
D. Examination of title

THIS IS THE END OF THE NATIONAL PORTION.

STATE PORTION

1. What is the intent of the Texas Real Estate Licensing Act?

   A. Provide laws that govern property transactions by Texas licensed real estate professionals who are practicing in Texas or another state
   B. Provide laws that govern real estate transactions and professionals in Texas
   C. Uphold rules created by the Texas government that align with federal real estate guidelines
   D. Provide guidelines that keep TREC in check

2. The state of Texas is a _____, which states property acquired by a married couple is equally owned by both spouses.

   A. Community property jurisdiction
   B. Joint custody state
   C. Common law state
   D. Joint tenancy

3. Which TREC form is used to report deficient conditions in a home?

   A. Notice to prospective buyer
   B. Property inspection form
   C. Seller's disclosure notice
   D. Public information request

4. A licensed real estate agent must renew their license every _____.

   A. 2 years
   B. 1 year
   C. 5 years
   D. 10 years

5. Who holds on to earnest money?

   A. An impartial third party
   B. The broker
   C. A salesperson
   D. The owner of the brokerage

6. What is definition of errors and omissions insurance?

   A. Insurance a principal is required to obtain when selling their home
   B. Insurance a potential buyer can obtain to cover misrepresentation caused by a broker
   C. Professional liability insurance that protects employees against claims made by clients
   D. None of the above

7. When is an IABS disclosure not required?

   A. Residential lease transactions
   B. Communication during an initial meeting
   C. When the licensee is also the principal
   D. During a lease to own sale

8. What is the maximum payment a party can receive from the Real Estate Inspection Recovery Fund?

   A. $25,000
   B. $50,000
   C. $12,500
   D. $10,000

9. A _____ is responsible for negotiating easement for lands being sought for development.

   A. Salesperson
   B. Right-of-way agent
   C. Broker
   D. Lawyer

10. Which is not a canon of professional ethics and conduct?

    A. Fidelity
    B. Integrity
    C. Illegal discriminatory practices
    D. Honor

11. What must a person do prior to filing a claim for payment from one of the recovery funds?

    A. A certified letter must be sent to the TREC license holder
    B. A lawsuit must be filed against the TREC license holder
    C. They must wait 90 days before filing a claim
    D. Mediation must occur between the client and the licensee

12. TREC requires _____ in earnest money contracts.

    A. Mediation
    B. Concessions
    C. Joint ventures
    D. Trust deeds

13. When can TREC investigate a licensee?

   A.   At random
   B.   When a written and signed complaint has been submitted
   C.   When verbal complaint by the brokerage has been submitted
   D.   None of the above

14. Which is an example of fraudulent misrepresentation?

   A.   When a party unknowingly makes a false statement
   B.   When an inspector makes a false statement
   C.   When an appraiser unknowingly makes a false statement
   D.   When a party makes an untrue statement of fact which induces the other party to enter a contract

15. Which is not a type of obsolescence?

   A.   Technological
   B.   Socio-economic
   C.   Legal
   D.   Aesthetic

16. Which is true about a real estate profession with an inactive license?

   A.   The licensee can still work on active contracts but cannot seek out new contracts
   B.   The licensee cannot conduct any real estate transactions
   C.   The licensee will lose their license if they do not activate it within 30 days
   D.   The licensee must wait 1 year to reactivate the license

17. _____ is required by sellers of previously occupied single-family residences and contains information regarding the property.

    A. Seller's disclosure notice
    B. Nonagency
    C. Exclusive right to sell
    D. Judicial foreclosure

18. The _____ is TREC's centralized customer service division.

    A. Administration and management services
    B. Reception and communication services
    C. Education and examination services
    D. Licensing and registration services

19. What is the purpose of residential service companies?

    A. To provide contracts for services related to maintenance of certain home systems
    B. To perform inspections of real property
    C. To provide contract services to real estate licensees
    D. To provide an estimate of a home or property's value

20. A _____ is an option for a renter to purchase a property during the lease contract term.

    A. Graduated rental lease
    B. Open-end mortgage
    C. Take-out financing
    D. Lease purchase agreement

21. What is a fitness determination test?

    A.   A test designed to see if a person is fit to be a Texas real estate licensee

    B.   A test to see if a person is physically fit enough to do the work required of a salesperson

    C.   A test a licensee needs to pass to open up their own brokerage

    D.   A test to determine the fitness of a TREC member

22. Which form is used to end a real estate contract in the state of Texas?

    A.   Contract amendment

    B.   Information about buyer's termination of contract

    C.   Notice of buyer's termination of contract

    D.   Notice of easements and right-of-way

23. The _____ is a professional trade association that provides services to its members.

    A.   Texas Real Estate Commission

    B.   Texas Association of Realtors

    C.   Texas Real Estate Licensing Act

    D.   Texas Broker-Lawyer Committee

24. What happens when a property with a homestead exemption is sold?

    A.   The homestead exemption transfers to the new owner

    B.   The homestead exemption follows the seller

    C.   The homestead exemption becomes null and void

    D.   None of the above

25. The _____ is used to pay final judgements against licensed inspectors.

A. Agreed judgment review
B. Real Estate Recovery Trust Account
C. Public information request
D. Real Estate Inspection Recovery Fund

26. What is the statutory period for adverse possession?

A. 3 years
B. 5 years
C. There are a few different potential statutory periods
D. 10 years

27. Which is not a type of real estate inspector?

A. Professional inspector
B. Property inspector
C. Real estate inspector
D. Apprentice inspector

28. _____ is a non-exclusive contract that uses multiple real estate agents to find a possible buyer.

A. Open listing
B. Exclusive right-to-sell listing
C. Exclusive agency listing
D. Multiple broker listing

29. What is a property valuation?

    A. How much a property will increase in value in a specified amount of years
    B. An informal appraisal completed by a real estate agent
    C. Assessment of a property's value that is based on factors such as location and condition
    D. The depreciation of property

30. Which is not a type of homestead exemption?

    A. School taxes
    B. Low income exemptions
    C. Disabled veteran homeowners
    D. Option percentage exemptions

31. Which of the following does not have to be disclosed to a renter by the landlord?

    A. The identity of anyone authorized to act on the behalf of the landlord
    B. The tenant's rights when a landlord fails to make necessary repairs
    C. Lead based paint concerns
    D. All of the above needs to be disclosed

32. Which document authorizes the broker to represent the seller?

    A. Listing agreement
    B. Assignment contract
    C. Purchase agreement
    D. Lease agreement

33. _____ is when there is more space than the market demands.

A. Demand market
B. Buyer's market
C. Seller's market
D. Leasing market

34. What does a client owe to a broker?

A. Indemnification
B. Compensation
C. The client does not owe anything to the broker
D. Both A&B

35. TRELA does not apply to which of the following?

A. State licensed attorney
B. On-site management of an apartment complex
C. Licensed real estate brokers and salesperson
D. TRELA applies to all of the above

36. The owner of a residential property dies 2 weeks after signing an exclusive right-to-sell agreement. The broker finds a buyer for the property, but the new administrator of the estate does not want to sell. Which statement is true?

A. The administrator is not required to sell the property or pay commission to the broker
B. The administrator can refuse to sell the property but must pay commission to the broker
C. The administrator is required to respect the wishes of the deceased owner
D. The agreement is between the broker and the residential property

37. Chapter 21 of the Texas Property Code, _____, is the inherent right the local government has to take private real estate property for public use.

    A. Actual eviction
    B. Suit for possession
    C. Eminent domain
    D. Condemnation

38. What are the four economic characteristics of land?

    A. Scarcity
    B. Permanence of investment
    C. Area preference
    D. All of the above

39. If a seller defaults on a contract, which of the follow can the buyer not do?

    A. Move into the property
    B. Terminate the contract
    C. Enforce specific performance
    D. Seek relief as provided by law

40. _____ is not a responsibility of a property manager.

    A. Manage daily complaints
    B. Obtain a listing for resale
    C. Maintain high occupancy
    D. Preserve the building

THIS IS THE END OF THE STATE PORTION.

Answer Key – National Portion

1.	D	21.	B	41.	D	61.	B	81.	A
2.	D	22.	A	42.	C	62.	D	82.	B
3.	B	23.	B	43.	B	63.	A	83.	C
4.	A	24.	A	44.	B	64.	B	84.	D
5.	D	25.	B	45.	B	65.	A	85.	A
6.	A	26.	D	46.	A	66.	B		
7.	D	27.	A	47.	B	67.	B		
8.	D	28.	A	48.	A	68.	A		
9.	B	29.	C	49.	A	69.	B		
10.	B	30.	C	50.	C	70.	C		
11.	A	31.	C	51.	C	71.	A		
12.	D	32.	D	52.	D	72.	C		
13.	B	33.	B	53.	A	73.	D		
14.	A	34.	B	54.	B	74.	D		
15.	B	35.	D	55.	B	75.	A		
16.	B	36.	B	56.	A	76.	C		
17.	C	37.	A	57.	D	77.	A		
18.	C	38.	C	58.	A	78.	C		
19.	D	39.	A	59.	C	79.	A		
20.	D	40.	D	60.	B	80.	D		

1.   **D) All of the above**

Commercial property includes mixed use buildings (e.g. retail store on the first floor, residences above) office buildings, hotels, retail stores, multifamily houses, industrial warehouses, and more.

2.   **D) Steering**

Steering is the act of guiding prospective buyers to specified settlement areas based on race, religion and other discriminatory factors.

3.   **B) Net lease**

This is a lease where the tenant pays rent and part of utilities fee and property taxes. The landlord is tasked with paying the utility bills and property taxes that are not covered by the tenant. This lease is common in commercial real estate.

4. **A) Lis Pendens**

    This is a legal notice that a lawsuit concerning a real estate property is pending. Usually involves a property title or claims of ownership interest. Details of a property whose title is in question are required to be filed at the county record to notify future buyers and lenders.

5. **D) Zoning Board of Appeals**

    The Zoning Board of Appeals is a board of select members that is given jurisdiction to hear and decide on appeals regarding zoning laws.

6. **A) Mortgage Banker**

    A mortgage banker is an individual who originates, closes and funds with his own funds or that of a company. Once a mortgage is originated it is either retained or sold to an investor. A mortgage banker has the power to approve or reject a mortgage and earns fees on the origination of a loan.

7. **D) Sheathing**

    Sheathing is a covering structure and acts as a case for the exterior of the home. Usually used to describe a boarding material that forms the roof, floor and walls. It provides a surface for other materials and strengthens weather resistance.

8. **D) Landlord**

    A security deposit is an amount equaling monthly rent that is paid to ensure rent will be paid and to cater for other responsibilities highlighted in the lease. Can also be used as security for unpaid rent and damages and is held onto by the landlord.

9. **B) Effective age**

    This is an estimate of a building age based on its utilities and the wear and tear. It could be the actual age or a little more or less than the actual age. This is dependent on maintenance, remodeling and removal of inadequacies. It is used to determine the remaining life of a building.

10. **B) Three years**

    Brokers are required by law to hold on to a copy of property files for a minimum of 3 years. This is to act as a proof in case of a dispute in the future. These include copies of all listings, deposit receipts, cancelled checks and trust records executed or obtained during the transaction.

11. **A) British Thermal Unit**

Defined as the amount of heat required to raise the temperature of one pound of water by one degree Fahrenheit. In the case of air conditioning, it is defined as the number of BTU per hour products that can be added or removed from the air.

12. **D) Habendum clause**

This is a legal agreement that involves the rights and interests of a property being transferred to a lessee. For a leased property there is a transfer of ownership and restrictions on the property. A purchased property is void of restrictions and only transfers ownership.

13. **B) Passive**

This is an income source that requires little to no daily input in order to yield returns.

14. **A) Ground lease**

This is a lease agreement where a tenant is allowed to develop a parcel of land during the lease period. On expiry of the lease, all improvements remain in the owner's custody. Land leases are often last between 50-99 with other agreement allowing for renewal.

15. **B) Building codes**

These are a set of regulations that are put in place to ensure design, construction, alteration and maintenance of structures is done according to the state's requirements. They aim at safeguarding the health, safety and welfare of the occupants.

16. **B) $335,051**

$325,000 / (1 - 0.03) = $335,051

17. **C) A fixture**

A fixture is any physical property that is permanently attached to real property (usually land). Fixtures are treated as a part of real property. Examples of fixtures are ceiling fans and TV mounts.

18. **C) Offsite improvements**

Offsite improvements are amenities that are not within the premise of the structure but are necessary to maximize the use of the property and ultimately increase the value of the property.

19. **D) Joint tenancy**

Joint tenancy is a form of ownership in which several people own a property together, each with equal shares and rights. If one of the owners in a joint tenancy dies, that owner's share in the property is automatically passed to the remaining owners.

20. **D) Preventive maintenance**

In order to maintain tenants and an acceptable return on an investment, routine checks and repairs have to be done. These are done to safeguard against failing which may incur losses to the property manager that arise due to cost of replacement.

21. **B) CERCLA**

The Comprehensive Environmental Response Compensation and Liability Act of 1980 was enacted in order to identify, investigate and facilitate cleanup of hazardous sites. The act is currently administered by the Environmental Protection Agency.

22. **A) A shared tenancy in which each holder has a distinct, separately transferable interest**

This type of ownership is characterized by ownership between two or more people who can have either equal or unequal shares. Unlike a joint tenancy, if an owner dies, the person's share is passed to his/her heirs and not distributed to the remaining owners.

23. **B) Cash flow**

This is the amount of profit retained after paying off all operating costs and repurposing amounts made in dividends for use in future repairs. To be able to profit from an investment, one must maintain a positive cash flow.

24. **A) A lien that arises without the property owner's consent**

Involuntary liens are placed by government facilities for unpaid taxes.

25. **B) Homestead property**

Homestead laws are laws that exist to ensure to protect owners from losing their home equity while filing for bankruptcy. Homestead property enables an individual to declare a portion of property as homestead to avoid forced sale.

26. **D) Special agent**

This is an agent engaged to perform a specific duty for a client. Their authority is limited to that particular task that translates in the expiry of the contract once the task is completed.

27. **A) Bundle of rights**

These are legal rights that are granted to a property buyer which include right to possession, control, exclusion, enjoyment and disposition. A property owner is automatically granted the bundle of rights. In a commercial property, different rights can be assigned to different parties.

28. **A) $1,000**

Violation of license laws may result in suspension of a license or a fine of not more than $1,000 paid to the Department of State. A reprimand is given together with the fine.

29. **C) 39 years**

After 39 years a commercial property is eligible for applying for value loss by depreciation in order to reduce property taxes levied

30. **C) Proration**

Proration occurs during corporate action to ensure all shareholders are treated fairly and a company does not deviate from its original target. Shareholders are offered equity or cash and required to elect one. Once the election is done, shareholders are compensated and if the shares or cash are not enough to satisfy the election each shareholder gets their due in both equity and cash.

31. **C) 7.48 gallons**

32. **D) Operating statement**

An operating statement is a financial statement that is done monthly and annually to document the expenses incurred and revenue gained. From the statement one can calculate the net profit or loss within the period.

33. **B) Condop**

This is a real estate building where the housing units are divided into co-op residential units and condos. They offer more flexible rules than a co-op. Condo units are retained or sold separately by the developer.

34. **B) General Agent**

This is an agent that is mandated to represent the principal in more than one affair.

35. **D) Usury**

These are laws that are laws set in place to protect borrowers from abusive lending such as imposing unusually high interest rates. Lenders usually target with little knowledge on the traditional loan system. An APR is usually set to protect buyers from being exploited by lenders.

36. **B) Leasehold**

This is a title on a property being leased and scheduled payments are made throughout the term of the lease. Improvements made within the property are either expensed or capitalized depending on their values.

37. **A) Mortgage**

A mortgage is a voluntary lien taken out to raise funds to buy a property. The lien is entered willingly and therefore possession of the property remains with the debtor.

38. **C) Tenancy in sufferance**

In this case, a tenant is granted the privilege to live within the premise before landlord decides to ask the tenant to vacate. Terms of the original lease must be met during this period of time. This type of tenancy can only be terminated by a written notice given not less than 30 days before the tenant is expected to move out.

39. **A) Yes**

There are no laws restricting a real estate salesperson from working multiple jobs.

40. **D) Private investors and government agencies that buy and sell real estate mortgages**

This is where home loans and servicing rights are bought within the market. Once a home loan is obtained, it is underwritten, financed and services by a lending facility. A lending facility sells loans to the secondary mortgage market in order to replenish loaning money.

41. **D) Rights granted to a property owner on the vertical space above the property**

The air space is subject to reasonable use by neighboring buildings and aircrafts. Like with property, air rights can be leased or sold.

42. **C) Co-broking**

This is a situation where two or more agents that are involved in the same the same transaction agree to work together in order to meet the needs of both parties. In this case, the agents are legally required to act in the best interest of the clients.

43. **B) Lease assignment**

A lease assignment is a legal arrangement where the landlord allows a tenant to assign another tenant to lease the apartment. The tenant is responsible for paying rent and utility fees directly to the landlord. In the case of a lease assignment, the previous tenant is held accountable for defaults in unpaid bills by the assignee.

44. **B) $2,000**

($200,000 * 0.12) / 12 = $2,000

45. **B) Closing costs**

These are the extra costs that are usually incurred by a home buyer on top the agreed upon price. They usually include title insurance, attorney fees and lender fees. These costs are negotiable but commonly paid by buyers.

46. **A) Common charges**

These are the monthly charges that are imposed on condo and condop tenants to cover common charges and amenities. They are usually cover maintenance of shared spaces and operation expenses of a building.

47. **B) Debt to income ratio**

This is a way lenders use to calculate the ability of a borrower to manage the monthly payments required in the settlement plan. Borrowers with a higher ratio have been established to experience struggles in meeting the monthly payments. 43% has been determined to be the highest ratio that can be offered credit.

48. **A) Down payment**

A down payment is an amount paid by the buyer to the seller to secure the property. A down payment is usually paid from the buyer's savings. Contrary to common belief, there is no set percentage of down payment that should be placed on a property

49. **A) Money deposited by the buyer to the seller to show interest in the purchase of a home**

This amount is deposited to give the buyer time to look into the title, sanction an appraisal and conduct an inspection of the property. This money can be returned to the buyer only in the case of a contract breach.

50. **C) Escrow**

This arrangement involves a third party that is neutral to the transaction. Usually used to secure payment in an account that can only be released on meeting of all the terms of the agreement. An escrow account is often used in transactions that involve large amounts of money such as real estate. A listing agent open an account and once the terms are signed upon by both the buyer and the seller, the deal is closed.

51. **C) Notice of termination**

This is a notice given to a tenant to end tenancy stating the reason for termination of tenancy, the date by which the tenant is required to vacate the premise and the legal implication of refusing to move.

52. **D) Notice to quit**

This is a notice given by the landlord regarding someone living in the home as a squatter. The notice usually states that the tenant is required to vacate the property within 10 days and the implications of failing to do so.

53. **A) Notice of cessation**

This is notice given by the contractor by the contractee to state that no work regarding construction has been done for a specified period of time. This notice is given in order to begin mechanical liens compensation.

54. **B) Home inspection**

They are an important part of the real estate transaction as one is able to identify the condition of the property being bought. Inspection of facilities such as plumbing, fixtures and foundation condition comes in handy in determining the value of the property.

55. **B) Convertible ARM**

This is a mortgage plan that allows an individual to benefit from the falling interest rates with the option of switching to a fixed-rate payment plan at a small fee. This switch can be made within the second to fifth year of the mortgage payment period.

56. **A) Delinquency**

This is a situation that arises where a borrower that is legally bound with the responsibility to make necessary payments on a loan or a bond interest foregoes paying the loan. Delinquency usually results in penalties depending on the type of loan and reasons behind failed payments.

57. **D) Federal Housing Administration**

This is United States Agency whose goal is to enable low income individual acquire mortgage loans. The agency approves and insures the lenders. An FHA loan requires a loan down payment and a credit score of at least 580.

58. **A) Consumer Financial Protection Bureau**

This is a regulatory agency that is tasked with the responsibility of overseeing the products and services offered to consumers by financial institutions. In the event of mishandling of a consumer, a complaint is filed to the CFPB for resolution.

59. **C) Multiple Listing Service**

This is a system employed by real estate broker that allows them to view each other's listings. Sharing the database amongst a group of brokers enables brokers to identify buyers for properties they are engaged in.

60. **B) Home warranty**

This is a contract made to ensure the cost of maintaining a household are met. It is put in place as a legal assurance that the property is fit for its intended purpose and meets the expectations of the buyer. It is usually taken to protect against expensive home repairs.

61. **B) Escalation clause**

This is a contract that allows a buyer to set a selling price but any offers higher than the stated price will automatically lead to an increase in the set price. This gives sellers an option to outbid each other and help in making the decision for the sale price.

62. **D) Notice of intent**

This is a non-binding proposal between a buyer and seller of a property to negotiate terms of a real estate transaction. It is usually detailed and lays key points on the weight of the transaction. It is usually used to determine the seriousness of the prospective buyer on the property.

63. **A) Appreciation**

This is the increase in the value of an asset over a period of time. It usually occurs due to increased demand or weakening supply.

64. **B) Biweekly mortgage**

This is a mortgage that requires a principal and interest payment plan every two weeks. It usually has a reduced interest rate throughout the lifespan of the loan.

65. **A) Addendum**

This is an attached document that is usually included as part of the contract during the preparation. It can act as an informal explanatory attachment or to indicate other requirements of the contract that have not been included in the main attachment.

66. **B) Cash out refinance**

This is where a homeowner refinances a mortgage for more than its value and withdraws the difference amount as cash. It is only possible to borrowers with a 20% equity on their mortgage.

67. **B) Department of Buildings**

In order to ensure that building codes are adhered to and construction and renovations are done by professionals, a building permit is required for any building or renovation project. A building permit is a go ahead issued by local government to a contractor to construct or remodel a building. It is issued to ensure that building codes are adhered to and standards are maintained.

68. **A) Closing**

This is the final stage of a real estate transaction. At this point, the date where contract becomes active is agreed on. On the closing date, the property is legally transferred from the seller to the buyer.

69. **B) Commission**

This is the percentage earned by a real estate agent for effort placed in facilitating the transaction. It is usually between 5-6% of the sales price and is paid by the seller on closing. It is usually split between the buyer's and seller's agent.

70. **C) Discount points**

Also referred to as mortgage points, these are fees paid directly to a lender by a homebuyer at closing time. They are usually paid in exchange for lower interest rates reducing monthly payments on the mortgage.

71. **A) Equal Credit Opportunity Act**

This act was enacted in 1974 and rules it unlawful for lenders to discriminate against loan applicants based on gender, race, age and religion.

72.   **C) A property sale is being handled without a real estate agent**

This phrase is used to declare that a property sale is being handled without a real estate agent. While using real estate agents to facilitate sale, some home sellers would rather avoid agents in order to save on the amount spent on commission. In this case the seller must disclose that they are not using an agent.

73.   **D) Settlement statement**

This is a document that is usually used to summarize expenses incurred during a loan translation and varies according to loan types. It is usually part of the closing package that must be reviewed and signed by the borrower when closing a loan. A comprehensive settlement statement is legally required for every loan.

74.   **D) Tax assessor**

An official whose responsibility is to determine the value of each taxable property in a region.

75.   **A) $220,000**

$88,000 / 0.4 = $220,000

76.   **C) Freehold estate**

An estate that has exclusive rights of the property for an undefined length of time. The three types of freehold estates are fee simple absolute, fee simple defeasible and life estate.

77.   **A) Signature of the grantee**

The grantee does not need to sign a deed. A deed needs to be in writing, must be signed by the grantor, the grantor must have the legal capacity to transfer the property, the grantor and grantee must be identified, the property must be described adequately, the deed must be legally delivered to the grantee and the grantee must accept the deed.

78.   **C) The owner of real estate who leases the property to another**

A person who grants a lease to someone else. This person is the owner of the real estate and leases it a lessee through an agreement.

79.   **A) When property is held by two or more parties**

It is an agreement in which two or more people own a property with equal rights and obligations. Joint tenancy is typically entered at the same time and through a deed. If one of the owners were to die their portion of the property would automatically pass to the survivors.

80.   **D) A document used when one party has taken out a loan from another party to purchase property**

It represents an agreement between the borrower and the lender in which the property is held in a trust managed by a third party until the borrower pays off the loan. The legal title of the property is transferred to the third party to hold. Trust deeds are used in place of mortgages in numerous states.

81.   **A) Fixity**

Also called investment permanence is property that takes a long time to pay for itself. It also refers to the fact that land cannot be moved but is in a fixed location.

82.   **B) The new property owner and tenant must honor all the terms of the original lease**

Property sold with an existing lease is still valid and it must be honored by both the new owner and the tenant.

83.   **C) Restrictive covenants**

Restrictive covenants is restriction on land use to ensure the value and enjoyment of adjoining land will be preserved. This clause limits what a tenant or owner can do with property.

84.   **D) Married couples**

Tenancy by the entirety is a type of concurrent estate in real property limited to married couples. Each spouse has an equal and undivided interest in the property and they mutually own the entire estate.

85.   **A) Certificate of occupancy**

A building inspector must issue a certificate of occupancy after the final inspection. It is a document issued by the local government or building department that states the building is in compliance with the building codes and is suitable for occupancy.

Answer Key – State Portion

1.	B	21.	A
2.	A	22.	C
3.	B	23.	B
4.	A	24.	A
5.	A	25.	D
6.	C	26.	C
7.	C	27.	B
8.	C	28.	A
9.	B	29.	C
10.	D	30.	B
11.	B	31.	D
12.	A	32.	A
13.	B	33.	A
14.	D	34.	D
15.	B	35.	C
16.	B	36.	A
17.	A	37.	C
18.	B	38.	D
19.	A	39.	A
20.	D	40.	B

1. **B) Provide laws that govern real estate transactions and professionals in Texas.**

    TRELA is enforced by TREC and helps protect the public from deceiving acts by brokers and salespersons.

2. **A) Community property jurisdiction**

    Texas is 1 of 9 states that practices community property jurisdiction. This rule states that property acquired during marriage needs to be divided if the couple decides to divorce.

3. **B) Property inspection report**

    TREC requires inspectors to report certain hazardous conditions. The conditions may not have violated building codes at the time of construction, but TREC considers them as hazardous.

4. **A) 2 years**

A licensee must renew their license every 2 years. A notice of renewal will be mailed to the licensee 90 days prior to the license expirations and a license cannot be renewed until the notice of renewal is received.

5. **A) An impartial third party**

The earnest money is held by an impartial third party like an escrow agent or a title company. This person or company holds onto the money until the transaction has closed.

6. **C) Professional liability insurance that protects employees against claims made by clients**

This insurance protects companies and employees against claims made by clients for inadequate work or negligent actions. Many clients may request proof of E&O insurance.

7. **C) When the licensee is also the principal**

IABS disclosure is not required when the licensee is acting solely as the principal, the residential lease is less than a year and there is no intent to sell, communication during an open house, or when the meeting is with a party is being represented by another licensee.

8. **C) $12,500**

The maximum payment from the real estate inspection recovery fund is $12,500 per transaction and $30,000 for all claims against one inspector.

9. **B) Right-of-way agent**

This agent is typically hired by a third party or government to acquire land. They negotiate easements and eminent domain processes for third parties.

10. **D) Honor**

The five cannons of ethics are consumer information form, illegal discriminatory practices, integrity, competency and fidelity.

11. **B) A lawsuit must be filed against the TREC license holder**

A lawsuit must be filed, and the plaintiff must obtain a civil judgement from the court against the TREC license holder. This also must happen within two years of the events that triggered the complaint. An abstract of judgement and writ of execution must also be obtained against the licensee.

12. **A) Mediation**

Mediation is required when the issues cannot be resolved through informal discussions. Parties must also find a mediation service and pay the cost for mediation.

13. **B) When a written and signed complaint has been submitted**

TREC can conduct a licensee investigation at its own motions or if they receive a complaint that is within 4 years of a contract or date of incident.

14. **D) When a party makes an untrue statement of fact which induces the other party to enter a contract**

Fraudulent misrepresentation also happens when a party does not believe the truth of the statement. A victim of fraudulent misrepresentation can claim rescission.

15. **B) Socio-economic**

Technological, legal, functional, aesthetic and economic are the different types of obsolescence. These types of obsolescence can cause depreciation to property even if the property is in good condition.

16. **B) The licensee cannot conduct any real estate transactions**

A license can be inactive for up to 6 months in the state of Texas. The licensee cannot conduct real estate transactions until the license is placed on act.

17. **A) Seller's disclosure notice**

The seller's disclosure notice is required by single family residence sellers and is used in conjunction with a contract for the sale of real property. The notice provides information regarding material facts and the physical condition of the property.

18. **B) Reception and communication services**

This division is responsible for receiving and responding to communications from consumers, license holders and applicants. The communications are in person, via email and telephone.

19. **A) To provide contracts for services related to maintenance of certain home systems**

Residential service companies or home warranty companies are licensed by TREC and typically provide contracts for services at the point of sale.

20.   **D) Lease purchase agreement**

This agreement states that part of the rent can be applied to an agreed purchase price of the lease property. This agreement must be prepared by an attorney.

21.   **A) A test designed to see if a person is fit to be a Texas real estate licensee**

This test makes sure that a licensee is not going to abuse their position and all licensees must meet TREC's qualifications of honest, trustworthiness and integrity. The test involves questions regarding criminal history and professional background, character references and a background check.

22.   **C) Notice of buyer's termination of contract**

This form is used when terminating a contract. The buyer tells the seller the intent to terminate the sale and that a form to terminate the sale is pursuant. The form will also list clauses that permit the termination.

23.   **B) Texas Association of Realtors**

A professional trade organization that, along with providing services to members, attempts to influence the rules and regulations of TREC. It is an advocate for its members and property owners.

24.   **A) The homestead exemption transfers to the new owner**

The sellers cannot keep the exemption and it transfers to the new owner. It is valid only when it is used as a primary residence by the owners.

25.   **D) Real Estate Inspection Recovery Fund**

This fund pays out judgements against licensed inspectors. TREC collects the fees for the fund from inspectors.

26.   **C) There are a few different potential statutory periods**

Texas has 3 different statutory periods which are dependent on the circumstance. The first is adverse possession after 3 years and must establish a color of title. The second is 5 years and the trespasser needs to show proof of cultivation of the land and payment of taxes. The third is 10 years and the trespasser must establish the standard elements of adverse possession.

27.   **B) Property inspector**

The apprentice and real estate inspector needs to be sponsored and indirectly supervised while the professional inspectors do not need sponsorship or supervision.

28. **A) Open listing**

This type of listing is an agreement where the listing is given to numerous brokers. The first broker to sell the home is given the commission.

29. **C) Assessment of a property's value that is based on factors such as location and condition**

The property valuation is carried out by a professional surveyor. Unlike an appraisal the property valuation is conducted by a licensed professional and typically have a fee involved.

30. **B) Low income exemption**

There are 7 different types of homestead exemptions. The different types are school taxes, county taxes, disabled veteran homeowners, optional percentage exemptions, optional 65 or older or disabled exemptions, and 65 or older and disabled exemptions.

31. **D) All of the above need to be disclosed**

The landlord is responsible for disclosing information to the tenant. This information is typically stated in the rental agreement.

32. **A) Listing agreement**

This document that contracts a real estate broker to find a buyer for the seller's property. This agreement gives a real estate agent authority to act as the owner's agent.

33. **A) Demand market**

This type of market typically forces a landlord to lower rent because the demand is low. When the demand is high, the landlord may be able to increase rent.

34. **D) Both A&B**

The client is owed the broker compensation as agreed up in the contract signed and indemnification. Indemnification protects the parties against losses from third party claims that are related to the contract.

35. **C) Licensed real estate brokers and salespersons**

TRELA regulations only apply to licensed brokers and salespersons. TRELA is designed to provide guidelines for the licensed agent and protect consumers.

36. **A) The administrator is not required to sell the property or pay commission to the broker**

Upon the death of a seller, the contract between a broker and the deceased owner is no longer valid. The same would occur if the broker were to pass away.

37. **C) Eminent domain**

Eminent domain allows the government to take property for public use. Texas law does not allow authorities to take property to enhance tax revenues or foster economic development.

38. **D) All of the above**

Scarcity, improvements, permanence of investment and area preference are economic characteristics of land. These characteristics affect the value as a product
.

39. **A) Move into the property**

The property still belongs to the seller if the seller defaults. The buyer has many options but moving into the property is not one of them.

40. **B) Obtain a listing for resale.**

The property manager is not responsible for obtaining a listing for resale. The property manager needs to be licensed if they wish to list, rent, negotiate or work on behalf of the landlord.

Resources

3.1 Finding a broker

Now that you've passed the exam, it's time to officially become an agent! Below is a list of companies and their websites to help you expedite your job search and help you start your journey in selling your first property!

CBRE – http://www.cbre.us/people-and-offices/corporate-offices/dallas-ft-worth
JLL – https://www.us.jll.com/en/locations?q=texas&o=&p=1&top=10
Cushman & Wakefield – https://www.cushmanwakefield.com/en/united-states/offices/houston
Transwestern – https://transwestern.com/location/dallas
Colliers International – https://www2.colliers.com/en/United-States/Cities/Houston
Marcus & Millichap – https://www.marcusmillichap.com/about-us/offices/dallas-texas
NAI Robert Lynn – https://nairl.com
Henry S. Miller – https://henrysmiller.com
Stream Realty Partners – https://streamrealty.com
Swearingen Realty Group – http://www.swearingen.com
Venture Commercial – https://www.venturedfw.com
The Retail Connection – https://theretailconnection.net
Newmark Knight Frank – http://www.ngkf.com/home/about-our-firm/global-offices/us-offices/dallas.aspx
Weitzman – http://www.weitzmangroup.com

Younger Partners – https://www.youngerpartners.com
Lincoln Property Co. – https://www.lpcdallas.com
EDGE Realty Partners – http://edge-re.com
STRIVE – https://www.strivere.com
Avison Young – https://www.avisonyoung.us/web/austin
Morrow Hill – https://www.morrowhill.com
Bradford Cos. – https://bradford.com
Rubicon Representation– https://rubiconrep.com
Mohr Partners Inc.– https://mohrpartners.com

3.2 Interviewing

Congratulations! You did get the interview. Now, just a little work and you can ace it!

First, start by going to all of the social media pages associated with your potential employer. Focus on several interesting things that they do and specialize in. Look at which type of listings they are showing on their pages and what types of neighborhoods they appear for listings. Look up the particular broker you are interviewing with and go to his/her LinkedIn page and learn more about her/him.

While you're looking at your potential employer's social media pages, take a look at your own. Are there any posts on your Facebook or other social media sites that need to be removed? Employers are looking at your pages. Anything inappropriate needs to go!

Real estate is all about creating a network of potential clients who trust that what you're selling to them will meet their needs. This means you must understand to differentiate between a client looking to buy a house to raise their newborn and a client who is looking for long term appreciation.

Try simulating cold calls by opening up random properties on Zillow or Trulia, studying them for 2 minutes, and then trying to sell your friend on these properties. They will most likely be asking similar questions to actual prospective buyers or sellers, so it's a very useful exercise in preparing yourself for the mock cold call during the interview.

In addition, study the geography of your broker's city to make sure you don't go in completely blind. Get familiar with the prices and trends in those areas and even take a tour. Drive or walk around and know the neighborhood like the back of your hand so you can impress the employer

On the day of the interview choose your outfit carefully. You should wear some type of suit and make sure your shoes are in good condition. Ask a friend to give you input on the clothes that make you look the most professional. Make sure you brushed your teeth, and your hair is neatly styled. Make sure you don't smell of smoke as most workplaces are smoke-free. No perfume or cologne – your new office may be perfume free. Never chew gum! You will not get the job!

When you arrive at the interview, always make sure to greet the receptionist. Every person you meet at your potential future employer is important! Make a good impression.

When you land the interview, it's important to have certain answers prepared to more commonly asked questions. First, let's look at general types of questions that you may be asked at any type of interview:

1. Tell me about yourself. This is not the time to talk about everything that happened to you from birth. This is an opportunity to show off a certain drive or characteristic or hobby that is special and helps to explain why you are seeking that particular job. For example, did you participate in a lot of team sports or a lot of clubs in high school or college? Did you work on volunteer projects that required you to meet a lot of new people of all ages and work with them and/or help them? The interviewer has your resume (Always bring extras with you!), so you do not have to spout off all of your previous education and positions. Devote just a sentence or two to that part of your answer.

2. What are your greatest strengths and weaknesses? This is a very tricky question. We all know our strengths; winning personality, gets along with everyone, good at math, good at negotiating, etc., but what about our weaknesses? Well, you certainly want to be honest but now isn't the time to confess all. Choose one. Do you take too long sometimes on a project because you want every detail to be perfect? Do you sometimes want to do something completely by yourself, but you really would be better off asking others for help? These are just two examples of weaknesses that won't sound like you are unprepared for your new job.

3. Where do you see yourself in 5 years? This seems pretty straightforward but be careful. The person interviewing you could be a manager. It is best not to say that you want his/her job. Instead, it may be better to say, I see myself expanding into new roles, doing what I do better, expanding my client base, becoming more successful, continuing my real estate education, and similar phrases.

4. Why did you choose our Company? Everyone asks this question. If you haven't gone to the Company's website, don't go to the interview. You should know everything about the Company and the local office where you are interviewing. You should know which type of real estate they specialize in, how long it's been in business, any recent mergers or expansions, the physical area it is licensed to practice in, and as much as you find on their website and Facebook page and other social media.

5. Why should I hire you and not the next person? This is your moment in the spotlight. Don't just say "pick me!!". Here is a sample: "All of my life, I have enjoyed working with people; when I worked at X company or volunteered at Y organization, I was able to get along with all types of people from children to the elderly. I also have been on teams or worked on teams, and I enjoy it greatly. I like to help people, and there is no bigger purchase than a home. I believe that I have the people skills and the real estate knowledge that I need to be a successful addition to your Company.

6. Why are you leaving your current job? This is not the moment to say how much you dislike your current manager or co-worker. Always be positive at your interview. You can talk about the lack of advancement opportunities, a salary freeze, future layoff being expected, change in your current employer's office location, or some other concrete reason. You can even say that you don't feel all of your skills are being utilized, and you want to use your new knowledge every day in your job.

7. Give me an example of a situation where you used teamwork to accomplish your goal. Even if you only work by yourself at your current job, look back to previous jobs and have the answer ready. If you don't have a job that matches, think about your volunteer activities at your children's school or at a community center or retirement village.

8. Would you rather work by yourself or as part of a team? This may be a good one to answer with a bit of vagueness. You can say that it depends on what the assignment might be. Do you have to give a major presentation to a commercial client? That might be a great time to ask for input and help as needed. Do you have to write a simple analysis of a problem? Maybe you feel more comfortable completing this on your own. You might want to say that it is very important to ask for feedback from co-workers and managers on projects and on small assignments when you have questions or reach a dead end.

9. What type of manager do you prefer? Do you prefer to work independently or to have more direction? This is always a tricky one as well. Make sure, once again, that you don't diss any of your former managers. A good response would be that you expect some direction from your manager. You feel that you know generally when you need help and would be sure to ask your manager for direction at those times. Also, you welcome all constructive feedback. It is very important to show that you are open to learning and open to change.

10. Why do you have gaps on your resume? Make sure you know the answer in advance to this question. Were you raising a family, taking care of an elderly parent, moving across the country due to a partner relocation, volunteering, etc. Whatever it is, make sure to answer this one without any hesitation and move on.

11. What is customer service? Be careful with this one. There are two types of customers – internal and external. Everyone you work with in your office is an internal customer; others are external. The same level of consideration should be given to both internal and external customers. Speak about how important it is to answer questions, do tasks that are needed, go above and beyond the average effort, and ask for help if you don't know the answers.

12. Are you organized? No one wants to admit they are disorganized. If you are going into real estate where there are mounds of paperwork and so many different elements to keep track with, let's assume that every person interviewing for this position must be organized!

13. What do you do when several people give you tasks to do, and it is clear to you that you will not be able to finish them on time?

14. Tell me about a time when you went above and beyond what was required? Hopefully, this will be an easy one to answer. Think about a suggestion you made to your manager to take on more work when a fellow employee was out sick or a time when you thought the presentation needed a special Powerpoint and you produced it.

15. Tell me about a time you had to deal with a difficult person and how you managed to diffuse the situation? You really need to think about this one in advance. If you can't think of a difficult person in your professional life, think about a friend of a friend or someone else. Always

acknowledge a difficult person's feelings and avoid arguing about strong opinions that impact an issue that isn't really that important.

16. If we offer you the position, how much notice do you have to give to your current employer? Be prepared to know the answer to this one. If you say that you can leave tomorrow, your future employer may not be pleased. It shows that you are not being loyal to your current employer by leaving them in the lurch. Two weeks is standard practice, but if you have a contract, be sure to read it.

Then, you will be asked more specific questions that are relevant to the real estate industry or this particular job. These include but are not limited to:

1. Why do you want to work in the real estate business?
2. This is a commission-based business, which means there is no ceiling to how much you can earn, but it also means there is no floor either. Are you open to this?
3. Let's go through a mock cold call together. I'll be the buyer, and you'll be the seller's agent.
4. How would you sell a property in a neighborhood you've never been to before?
5. A couple is looking to buy their first home. What kind of houses would you suggest?
6. A seasoned investor is looking for investment properties. By coincidence, the Independence Hall is for sale and you are the seller's agent. Pitch it to them.
7. A retiree is looking to sell their house. He is unsure about whether it's a good time to sell it. Explain to them why it is a good time to put the property on the market.

Be prepared to answer technical questions you may have studied for your exam such as:

1. What is the difference between a joint tenancy and a tenancy by the entireties?
2. What is the difference between a cooperative and a condominium?
3. Why is title insurance important?
4. Why would a buyer agree to lease back to a seller?
5. What are the duties of a buyer's agent?
6. What is a tax credit opposed to a tax deduction?
7. What is an easement?
8. Why would someone want to partition property, and what does this mean?
9. When would there be a lien on real estate?
10. What happens at settlement?
11. Why would a homeowner agree to finance a second mortgage for the buyer?

At the end of an interview, the interviewer will always ask if you have any questions. It is never a good idea to say, "No"! Here are some suggestions:

1. If I work here full time, what would be a range of the commissions I could expect in the first year?
2. What type of commission structure is there? Are commissions paid immediately upon closing? What types of fees am I required to pay out-of-pocket? Do I pay any advertising, computer, or other fees?
3. How often would I normally be assigned floor duty? If I answer the phone while on floor duty, do I get that listing?

4. How many open houses would I normally attend a month?
5. What is your hiring process timewise?
6. Do you pay for continuing education?
7. Although I know there isn't a truly "typical" day, what kinds of activities will I be performing during my first few weeks on the job?
8. When I attend my first settlement, will someone more senior come with me to the closing?
9. Will I attend all of the inspections for my listings?
10. What are the types of problems that arise at settlement?
11. Do you give out a list of mortgage brokers to clients?
12. How many people work in this office?
13. Is there coordination with other nearby offices – both this brand and others?
14. Do you provide a list of mortgage brokers to the buyer?

When you are finished with your interview, make sure to thank the interviewer, ask for her/his card, and thank the receptionist before you leave. Every impression counts! When you arrive home, if you really do want to work at that office, within 24 hours write a short email thank you note to your interviewer. If you don't hear back within a week, you can send a brief follow-up e-mail expressing your continuing interest in the position.

Made in the USA
Coppell, TX
27 July 2020